Motorbooks International
WARBIRD HISTORY

B-17
Flying Fortress

William N. Hess

*To the memory of
the Skipper, Ted, Mac, Gene, and Smitty–
the men with whom I went to combat.*

First published in 1994 by Motorbooks International Publishers & Wholesalers, PO Box 2, 729 Prospect Avenue, Osceola, WI 54020 USA

The information in this book is true and complete to the best of our knowledge. All recommendations are made without any guarantee on the part of the author or Publisher, who also disclaim any liability incurred in connection with the use of this data or specific details

We recognize that some words, model names and designations, for example, mentioned herein are the property of the trademark holder. We use them for identification purposes only. This is not an official publication

Motorbooks International books are also available at discounts in bulk quantity for industrial or sales-promotional use. For details write to Special Sales Manager at the Publisher's address

Library of Congress Cataloging-in-Publication Data Available

ISBN 0-87938-881-1

On the title page: A lineup of eleven of the twenty B-17Cs destined for the Royal Air Force in England. This photo was made at McChord Field, Tacoma, Washington, before the aircraft departed for the United Kingdom. *Boeing*

On the front cover: *Mary Ruth*, a B-17F, leads the 91st Bomb Group on a mission to hit targets in France, May 1943. *USAF via Jeff Ethell*

On the back cover: Top, a formation of B-17s over England. *via Jeff Ethell*. Lower left, a B-17 from the 100th Bomb Group that returned from its mission after having most of its tail blown off. Lower right, Royal Air Force B-17s. *Boeing.*

On the frontispiece page: *Roundtrip Jack* flew with the 385th Bomb Group.

Printed in Hong Kong

Contents

Acknowledgments

There are a number of people I would like to thank for material, photos, and favors that greatly aided me in writing this book. In particular, I owe a debt to my fellow historian Russell Strong, of the 306th Bombardment Group, for permission to quote from his history, *First over Germany,* and for many of the excellent photos that he provided. Mike Chambers loaned me his father's invaluable diary and photo albums from his B-17 days in the Pacific. John Mitchell, author of *On Wings We Conquer,* gave me permission to quote, and also provided rare photographs. The Rev. James Good Brown gave me permission to quote from his history of the 381st Bombardment Group, and C. B. Rollins, Jr., loaned me a copy of his 385th Bombardment Group book and valuable photographs. I would also like to thank the Boeing Corporation, John Bardwell, Jeffrey Ethell, Robert Gill, Tom Ivie, J. Griffin Murphey III, and Warren Thompson for their generous assistance with photographs for the book.

Introduction

When my editor, Greg Field, asked me if I would like to do a book on the Boeing B-17 it was almost like being asked to go home again. I fully realize that after so many years have passed you can't *really* go home again, but your memory can.

I grew up in an oil patch about forty-five miles from Barksdale Field, Louisiana (now Barksdale Air Force Base), and was privileged to see practically all of the different aircraft of the US Army Air Corps from 1932 onward. Their fighters and attack planes used to use some of the oil derricks for pylons, and they had a ball enjoying their own aerial circus of the 1930s. Barksdale was not a bomber base in those days, so I didn't get to see many of the multiengine aircraft, but it was always a great thrill to see the early Boeing B-17s fly over my home. I think that one of the most memorable sights I ever witnessed was watching the Boeing B-15 with a Boeing B-17 on each wing passing over one Sunday afternoon at about 1,000ft.

When I was assigned to a B-17 crew in 1944, it was once more a thrill and led to experiences that I would not want to live through again, but that I wouldn't take a million dollars for. To all of us who flew combat in its interior, the Fortress was a queen of the sky. The B-17 graced the sky with its beauty, and its formations made unforgettable sights that I can still see if I close my eyes. No truer legion ever charged than did the airborne attackers who unwaveringly entered the black fields of flak to carry out their mission. While many Fortresses fell, hundreds more brought their shattered airframes and wounded crews home where others might have failed.

I trust that in these pages I have painted just a little of the overall picture of the Fortress in combat. Writing this book brought back a lot of memories, and I hope that those readers who have experienced this story will find it accurate and informative. For those who seek to further their knowledge of the queen of the sky, I hope I have provided you with a valuable addition.

Chapter 1

The Flying Fortress

In May of 1934 the US Army Air Corps requested bids on Project X, which would comprise a bomber capable of carrying a bomb load of 2,000lb and possess a range of 5,000 miles. Boeing Airplane Company and the Glenn L. Martin Company submitted bids that resulted in Boeing Model 294 being ordered in 1935. The four-engine aircraft would be considered gigantic by 1935 standards, with a wingspan of 149ft and a length of 87ft 7in. The original request was that a 1,000hp engine be utilized, but the only thing available at the time was a Pratt and Whitney 850hp Twin Wasp. The original Air Corps designation of the aircraft XBLR-1 was changed to XB-15 before its completion.

The Air Corps issued another request in April of 1934 for a multiengine aircraft that would carry a 2,000lb bomb load for not less than 1,020 miles and if possible, 2,200 miles at a speed of 200 mph and possibly as high as 250mph. A flyable prototype was to be available not later than August 1935.

In August 1934, Boeing set out to build the prototype of design Model 299. Their board of directors approved a sum of $275,000 to build the aircraft. The aircraft had all-metal construction, with a conservative semi-monocoque fuselage with a forward gun turret in the extreme nose. The pilot and copilot were seated side by side in conventional commercial airline configuration. The bomb bay had

a capacity for 4,800lb of bombs. The radio room was a separate compartment aft of the bomb bay. Aerial gunners were provided with blisters on each side of the rear fuselage and another blister in the belly aft of the radio room. Full arma-

A Y1B-17 flies over cloud cover with Mount Rainier in the background. Boeing

ment consisted of five machine guns. The Model 299 was powered by four Pratt & Whitney R-1690 radial engines each developing 750hp.

The name "Flying Fortress" was coined by Dick Williams, a reporter for the *Seattle Times* who gave this name to Model 299 when it was rolled out displaying its colorful five machine-gun installations. Boeing quickly recognized the value of the title and had it copyrighted.

The first flight test was carried out on July 28, 1935, with Boeing chief test pilot Les Tower at the controls. The flight test program lasted only three weeks and consisted of seven flights totaling 14 hours and 5 minutes.

Following the company test program the Model 299 took off for Wright Field, Ohio, on August 20, 1935. The aircraft flew the 2,100 mile trip in only 9 hours and 3 minutes–an amazing ground speed of 233mph. The performance of the aircraft completely stole the show from Douglas' new B-18, which was essentially a bomber version of the DC-2 transport and Martin's worked-over, obsolete B-10.

On October 30, 1935, with Army Air Corps chief test pilot Ployer Hill at the controls and Les Tower flying as an observer, the aircraft took off on a second evaluation flight. Unfortunately, Hill forgot to take off the control locks. The aircraft took off and started to climb, then nosed over and plunged to the earth. Hill was killed in the crash and Tower succumbed to injuries a few days later.

The aircraft was not a complete loss, but the crash did dash the hopes that Boeing had for a sizeable contract. The bulk of orders for a new Army Air Corps bomber went to Douglas for the B-18.

Boeing was finally granted a contract on January 17, 1936, for thirteen aircraft to be designated YB-17. A number of changes were made on the aircraft from the original Model 299. The most significant was the change of engines. The new aircraft was fitted with Wright R-1820-39 Cyclone engines which developed 850hp. The first flight of the revised aircraft was made on December 2,

The gigantic Boeing B-15 was not a predecessor to the B-17. Its development was parallel, and it did not fly until 1937. Only one B-15 was built. It had a 149ft wing span and was 87ft, 7in in length. Its Pratt & Whitney 850hp engines were just not powerful enough for its size. Boeing

The nose turret was deleted on the Boeing B-17B. Superchargers were installed for the Wright Cyclone R-1820 engines. Boeing

Next page
The gun blisters were eliminated on the Boeing B-17C. In place of the ventral blister was a new bathtub ventral gun position. Boeing

11

A B-17B in all its shiny glory at rest as a heavy overcast moves in. Boeing

A B-17B of the 2nd Bomb Group. This aircraft was named Flagship *and was undoubtedly a lead aircraft for this famous 1930s unit.* Boeing

1936, with an Air Corps crew at the controls. The bombers were delivered to the 2nd Bomb Group at Langley Field, Virginia, where they served well and made many historic flights in the aircraft while compiling a record 9,293 accident-free hours.

While the 2nd Bomb Group was making record good-will flights to South America and attracting all kinds of attention to the B-17, there were those in Congress who were opposed to putting so much money into very large aircraft. Douglas continued to get contracts for B-18s, while the only thing new that Boeing came up with was the Y1B-17A, which was utilized to develop turbo-superchargers on the aircraft. Although not fully realized at the time, the work being done on superchargers would have great effect on later B-17 models.

In August 1937, Boeing got the first installment of contracts for the B-17B. Eventually, thirty-nine aircraft of this designation would be built. The primary change in this model was the elimination of the rotating nose turret, which was replaced with a bombardier's flat-glass aiming window, a larger rudder, and improved engines.

Even up until the outbreak of World War II in Europe, there was constant opposition from the Air Corps regarding the price of the B-17 and the desirability of the aircraft. At one time it appeared that no further contracts would be granted to Boeing. It was not until September 20, 1939, while Poland was being overrun by Germany, that the Army Air Corps contracted for thirty-eight B-17Cs. This new model eliminated the glass blisters on the aircraft and put the waist gunners behind a flat, tear-shaped opening. The belly gun position had a bathtub-type installation whereby the gunner could kneel and fire downward. In addition, the first self-sealing fuel tanks were fitted into the wings. Twenty B-17Cs went to England where they saw combat with the Royal Air Force (RAF).

The first B-17Ds were contracted in April 1940. These aircraft were originally to have been equipped with Sperry upper and lower gun turrets, but these turrets were still in the testing stage and were not installed in the aircraft. Instead, the aircraft got cowl flaps and dual gun installations in the radio room and in the belly. Most of the B-17Ds would see action in the Pacific, from the Pearl Harbor attack up until the time that most of them were lost in combat or associated operations.

As desperate as the Army Air Corps was for additional B-17s, when the contract came up for the sorely needed B-17E, which incorporated crucial improvements, it was held up in the US War Department for overpricing until August 30, 1940. The primary changes to the E model were in armament. The B-17E had a Sperry power turret just aft of the flight deck, a remote twin gun turret in the belly, and most significantly, a repositioned tail gun in the completely redesigned tail structure. The new tail, rudder, and dorsal fin drastically changed the look of the aircraft. A total of 512 B-17Es were contracted. A major change was implemented starting with the 113th B-17E when the Sperry ball turret was substituted for the remote turret, which had proved to be unsatisfactory.

The B-17E saw action in the Pacific, England, and North Africa, and was the real combat pioneer Flying Fortress. With the aircraft in great demand it was only natural that large quantities would be ordered. In fact, the orders were so large that when the B-17F began production, some orders were farmed out. The B-17F was basically the B-17E with over 400 small modifications. Boeing built 2,300 examples of the model in Seattle while another 500 were built in Burbank, California, by Lockheed/Vega. Douglas built 604 B-17Fs at Long Beach, California.

The biggest visible difference between the E and F model was the new one-piece, molded, clear plastic nose cone on the B-17F. As with the E model, there were four sockets for .30 caliber guns. With the Fortresses taking scores of vicious nose-on attacks over Europe, it was only natural that numerous field modifications would be made. The primary goal was to get more than one .50 caliber gun in the nose. Some units installed small window-type gun positions while others came up with the cheek type that would be standard equipment on the B-17G.

The B-17F also had new fuel tanks installed in outer wing panels which became known as "Tokyo tanks," and added another 1,100 gallons to the fuel capacity. Larger paddle-type propeller blades were fitted to give the engines more "bite" at high altitude.

The final and largest model of the Fortress was the B-17G. Like the F model, they were built at three factories. The totals were 4,035 in Seattle, 2,250 at Burbank, and 2,395 at Long Beach. The most welcome addition on the G model was the twin .50 caliber guns mounted in the chin turret beneath the bombardier's station. Many of the G models received a Cheyenne tail gun position which was installed at the United Air Lines modification center in Cheyenne, Wyoming. This gave the tail gunner a more comfortable bicycle seat and an optic head gun sight rather than the old ring and post. Waist windows were staggered and covered with plexiglass, eliminating the "butt bumping" by the waist gunners and the frigid air blast from the open windows.

There were other modifications of the Fortress that saw little or limited use. One major design variant was made when Lockheed/Vega built one model fitted with Allison V-1710-89 engines. The model was designated XB-38 and made its initial flight on May 19, 1943.

In an effort to assist the Fortress formations in their fight against the Luftwaffe before fighter escorts came along, twenty or more B-17Fs were converted to YB-40 escort gun ships. These Fortresses had chin turrets, a twin .50 caliber gun turret in the radio room, and twin gun installations in the waist positions. If cheek guns were installed, the aircraft carried at least fourteen .50 caliber guns. These modified ships were used on some Eighth Air Force missions, but it was found that the YB-40s could not keep up with the regular B-17s in formation, particularly after the B-17s had dropped their bombs. The idea was abandoned after nine missions.

B-17C assigned to the test section at Wright Field, Ohio. Ethell

16

Another B-17C in shiny splendor while assigned to Wright Field, Ohio. Ethell

B-17E in war colors. Its new olive-drab paint job shows up well against the clouds. Ethell

A Boeing B-17B that belonged to the 2nd Bomb Group at Langley Field, Virginia. This unit pioneered the virtues of the aircraft. US-AAF

This shiny new B-17D featured self-sealing fuel tanks, a new electrical system, and more armor. The B-17D was the first Flying Fortress model to see combat when it was used against the Japanese in 1942. Boeing

Brand-new B-17Cs on the hardstands outside the Boeing factory. Note how the lack of gun blisters gives the C-model sleeker lines.
Boeing

The B-17E was a completely new aircraft. The tail was redesigned and a tail gunner's position was added. It featured a Sperry top turret behind the flight deck and a remotely operated turret in the belly. Boeing

A Boeing B-17F in full war paint. With the Sperry ball turret and new plexiglass one-piece nose, the Flying Fortress was finally ready for war. This aircraft is from the 390th Bomb Group, Eighth Air Force. USAAF

This B-17G from the 91st Bomb Group, Eighth Air Force, features the chin turret in the nose and the improved tail gunner's station with an optical gun sight. Havelaar

The most heavily armed Fortress was the YB-40 which carried fourteen .50 caliber guns. The YB-40 was much more heavily armed than the standard B-17F from which it was modified. The YB-40 was given a chin turret, a power turret in the radio room and twin .50s in the waist windows. Boeing

Chapter 2

Royal Air Force Fortresses

In early 1941, the British Purchasing Commission accepted twenty Boeing B-17Cs for duty with the RAF. It was thought that with the aircraft's ability to operate at high altitude and with its speed and armament, it might be able to operate over Europe in daylight. The aircraft was not fitted with the secret Norden bombsight, and the RAF had to settle for one made by Sperry.

The first Forts began to arrive in England in May of 1941 and were assigned to No. 90 Squadron, which went in training on the aircraft at once. The aviators seemed quite pleased with the Fortress I, as it was called, and were eager to put it in action. The only real problems they encountered during their training was with the oxygen system and the cold weather. They were forced to change the oxygen system, and also came up with a serviceable electrically heated suit.

On July 8, 1941, three Fortress I aircraft took off on their first operation mission which was to bomb the docks at Wilhelmshaven, Germany. One aircraft was forced to salvo its bombs because of mechanical troubles, and a second aircraft had its bombs hang up over the target. The third Fortress dropped its bombs over the target with unknown results. Two of the aircraft sighted Messerschmitt Bf 109s climbing, but got up to 32,000ft and the enemy was not able to climb up to them. It was well that

they did not, for all the Fortress guns were frozen solid.

All through the summer of 1941, No. 90 Squadron mounted very high altitude missions against various targets. Most resulted in little or no damage to the enemy. It turned out that the bombsight

Fortress I airborne in service with No. 90 Squadron, RAF. Boeing

they were using was not accurate for such high-altitude bombing, and the aircraft was experiencing various other

A Fortress I on a test flight before leaving for England. Note that the rudder and vertical stabilizer have received camouflage paint while the balance of the aircraft is shiny silver. Boeing

problems resulting from the extreme cold at high altitudes.

For all practical purposes, operations ended for No. 90 Squadron, and the Fortress I aircraft in late September

1941. A number of the surviving aircraft were sent to North Africa where they flew some bombing missions against enemy shipping in the Mediterranean. The Fortress I had not been successful for

*A Boeing Fortress I in full camouflage paint.
The one operationsl squadron with the RAF,
No. 90 Squadron, had all sorts of troubles
with the aircraft, primarily due to freezing
temperatures in their attempt at high altitude
bombing. Boeing*

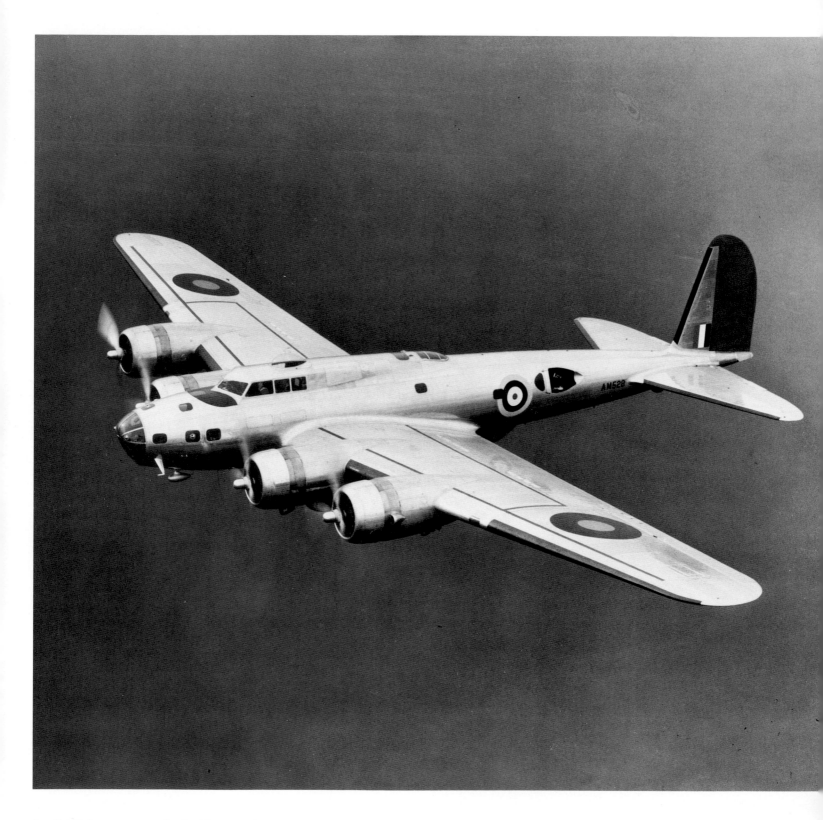

the RAF, but a great deal of knowledge was learned about the aircraft, and this knowledge was put to good use by the US Army Air Forces when it went to war with the Fortress.

The RAF received Boeing B-17Es and Gs later on in the war, and they served in Coastal Command where they did yeoman duty escorting ships and going after German U-boats. The Fortresses of Coastal Command were credited with the destruction of twelve U-boats before the end of the war.

Another in-flight photo of AM528. The Fortress I was undergunned, without self-sealing fuel tanks and the US Army Air Corps would not permit the secret Norden bomb sight to accompany the aircraft. Boeing

Chapter 3

The Pacific

The war did not come to the B-17 in the Pacific. Rather, the B-17 flew into it headlong. As part of the buildup in the Philippine Islands, an additional sixteen Fortresses were to stage through Hawaii in late November 1941. These aircraft came from the 38th Reconnaissance Squadron at Albuquerque, New Mexico, and the 88th Reconnaissance Squadron at Fort Douglas, Utah. Their departure was delayed by modifications and weather that held them in California. Army Chief of Staff Gen. George Marshall became alarmed at the delay and had Gen. H. H. Arnold, Army Air Corps chief of staff, get them going.

When the commander of the B-17 flight, Maj. Truman H. Landon, asked General Arnold why they weren't carrying ammunition if their departure was so urgent, Arnold told him they didn't need the extra weight. The second leg of the trip would be the dangerous one, and they could pick up ammunition for their guns in Hawaii.

As the flight prepared to leave Hamilton Field, California, two of the B-17s experienced engine trouble and were held over. Another Fortress had problems and did not take off, and a fourth aborted once it was airborne. All total, four B-17Cs and eight B-17Es departed for Hawaii.

The long flight was uneventful, and they had no trouble locating the island. Capt. Richard H. Carmichael called the tower at Hickam Field, but the reply was garbled and could not be understood. Shortly afterward a flight of fighter aircraft was spotted and the crews on the B-17s thought they were coming out to greet them. Suddenly, the fighter aircraft attacked the Fortresses and the pilots had to take immediate evasive action. They had flown right into the Japanese attack on Pearl Harbor on December 7, 1941!

Lt. Robert H. Richards tried to land his B-17C at Hickam, but he encountered so many Japanese attacks he aborted the landing and headed out to sea. He finally attempted a downwind landing at Bellows Field, but came in too fast and ran off the runway into a ditch. Zeroes then repeatedly strafed the aircraft and left it in an unflyable condition. Three of the crew were wounded.

Capt. Raymond T. Swenson managed to land his aircraft at Hickam, but a strafing Zero hit the flare box in the middle of the aircraft and it burned in two. The crew got out safely except for Lt. William R. Schick, the flight surgeon traveling with them, who was mortally wounded.

The four other aircraft of the 38th Reconnaissance Squadron managed to get down safely at Hickam.

The 88th Reconnaissance Squadron met much the same opposition as the 38th. Captain Carmichael and Lt. Harold Chaffin passed up Hickam and landed at a small auxiliary field at Hal-eiwa. Lt. Frank P. Bostrom tried to get in at Hickam, but finally gave up and flew to the northern part of the island where he landed on the Kahuku golf course. Two more Fortresses finally got in to Hickam safely between Japanese attacks. The last Fortress was reported to have originally landed at Wheeler Field, but it later wound up at Hickam. Fortunately, only two B-17s out of the flight of twelve were destroyed.

Of twelve B-17Ds already stationed at Hickam Field, five were destroyed in the attack by the Japanese.

At Clark Field in the Philippines nineteen B-17s were still on the base. A number of Fortresses had been sent south to Del Monte on Mindanao for safety. When news of the attack on Pearl Harbor came on December 8 (Philippine time), Col. Eugene Eubanks was called in for a conference with Gen. Douglas MacArthur, leaving Maj. David Gibbs in charge at Clark. Lt. Hewitt Wheless had taken off earlier that day on a reconnaissance mission over Formosa to investigate the Japanese build-up. Shortly after the alert there was a report of approaching enemy aircraft, so Gibbs ordered the B-17s into the air.

The most puzzling question that has mystified everyone is why MacArthur didn't order a strike on Formosa by the B-17s once he learned of the attack on Pearl Harbor. It has been said that he,

A line-up of B-17Ds at Port Moresby, New Guinea, on their way to the Philippines in September 1941. Wallach

Capt. Colin Kelly, who became America's first World War II hero when he saved his crew over the Philippines. He stayed at the controls of the crippled B-17 until his crew could bail out. Kelly died in the crash. USAAF

like the US administration, was waiting for the Japanese to make the first move. Likewise, Gen. Louis Brereton, commander of the Army Air Forces in the Philippines, was awaiting the return of his reconnaissance aircraft and no one ordered the strike.

Once the Fortresses were low on fuel Major Gibbs had them land, and then told them to go to lunch and await orders at their aircraft. Three crews were ordered on a photo mission over Formosa, and they were readied for takeoff. As the three B-17s began their takeoff roll, the first bombs began to fall on Clark Field. All three of these Fortresses were destroyed on the field. Few of the B-17s had been damaged by the bombing, but then the Zero fighters came down to strafe. When they had finished, twelve B-17s were destroyed and five were damaged. When Lieutenant Wheless returned from Formosa and another B-17 that had been on patrol over the eastern side of the island of Luzon landed at Clark, they were the only two serviceable B-17s left at the base.

The next morning, some of the B-17s from Del Monte came up to Clark and were sent out in an attempt to find a Japanese task force heading for Luzon, but failed to find it. Lieutenant Wheless took off from Clark Field in an attempt to bomb the invasion fleet, but an electrical failure forced him to abort the mission.

B-17s of the 19th Bomb Group flew the first American bombing missions of the war on December 10, 1941. Capt. Cecil Combs led a flight of five Fortresses attacking the Japanese invasion fleet in Lingayen Gulf. They dropped loads of 100lb bombs and reported hits on a transport.

Four B-17s that came up from San Marcelino landed at Clark Field to be bombed up to attack the Japanese invasion fleet. Maj. Emmett O'Donnell and Lt. George E. Schaitzel took off with loads of eight 600lb bombs, but Capt. Colin Kelly and Lt. G. R. Montgomery were forced to depart with partial bomb loads because of an air raid alert.

Major O'Donnell dropped his bombs on enemy vessels off Vigan north of Lingayen Gulf, but got no hits. Lieutenant Montgomery headed for Vigan and he, too, missed with all of his bombs. However, Montgomery returned to Clark, got another load of bombs, and returned to the Vigan area where he got hits on a Japanese transport.

Captain Kelly had only three 600lb bombs aboard, but went north to Aparri where a second enemy invasion force was landing. His first two bombs missed, but a third got a direct hit on an enemy cruiser. Kelly's crew reported the ship sunk.

As Kelly headed back to Clark, his Fortress came under attack from Japanese Zeros. They started a fire in the bomb bay and killed engineer-gunner Sgt. J. W. Delehanty. The enemy fighters continued to make passes at the bomber and started a fire in a wing tank. The B-17C that Kelly was flying was not equipped with self-sealing tanks. Kelly stayed at the controls until all of his crew could bail out. By this time, Kelly was too low to bail himself out and the aircraft exploded. Kelly's body was found near the wreckage with an unopened parachute.

With the rapid fire victories of the Japanese, the American public was desperate for something that would boost their morale. Capt. Colin Kelly would become its first hero. News releases told of his B-17 bombing and sinking of a Japanese battleship. He then saved the lives of all his crew by his self-sacrifice, for which he was posthumously awarded the Distinguished Service Cross and was lauded by President Franklin Roosevelt.

The last real Philippine bombing mission by the 19th Bomb Group was flown on December 14 against enemy shipping in Legaspi Bay. Six B-17s were assigned to the mission. Lt. James Connally was to lead the mission, but he blew a tire. Lt. Lee Coats then took over the lead, but was forced to abort because of engine trouble. He was soon followed by Lieutenant Ford, who also experienced engine trouble. Lieutenant Wheless also had engine trouble, but dropped down in altitude and was able to get his bad engine running again.

Lt. Jack Adams dropped his bombs on enemy shipping and was immediately jumped by six Zeros. He sought cloud cover, but the Zeros hung on. Two of his engines were shot out and two crew members were wounded. Adams successfully crash-landed his Fortress in a rice paddy on Masbate. Adams got out of the Philippines, but his crew were pressed into service as infantrymen.

Lt. Elliot Vandevanter made three bombing runs over the enemy shipping, but was unable to see the results. He returned to Del Monte without incident. Lieutenant Wheless was intercepted by Zeros before he got to his target. Two of his gunners were wounded and his radio operator, Private First Class Kellin, was killed. Wheless' bombardier dropped the 600lb bombs and Wheless went into evasive action. He managed to land his badly damaged aircraft on a small strip at Cagayen, flat tires and all.

With the loss of two more B-17s, the 19th Bomb Group had been reduced from thirty-five to fifteen B-17s. All of the surviving Fortresses were located at Del Monte, but now that the enemy had discovered the base it was imperative that they be moved. A strafing raid cost the group another B-17 before they began their departure for Australia on December 17. The few missions that the surviving Fortresses would fly in the Philippines would be flown from Batchelor Field in Australia, and staged through Del Monte.

The loss of the Philippines was now inevitable, and the surviving bombers, plus a handful that had arrived with the 7th Bomb Group, took up the fight in Java. By the end of December, the ma-

The crew of B-17 Daylight Limited, *which had to crash-land in Mareeba after an August 26, 1942, mission to Milne Bay.* Wallach

The famous B-17D Swoose *on its way home. It flew bomb missions with the 19th Bomb Group and became Gen. George Brett's aircraft. It was named for half-swan, half-goose, as it was rebuilt from two different B-17Ds.* Wallach

A B-17E at Charleville, Australia, in 1942 after the Philippines and Java had been lost to the rapidly advancing Japanese forces. Giroux

The Aztec's Curse *was flown by Capt. W. E. Chambers of the 26th Bomb Squadron during the Guadalcanal campaign.* Chambers

jority of bombers were in Java where they flew a limited number of missions against the enemy invaders, but with little success. It was too little too late to combat the overwhelming forces of Japan. By the first of March 1942, it was all over in Java.

The few aircraft that survived Java retreated to Australia. Bombing missions were then flown against new targets by the 7th and 19th Bomb Groups. The enemy was in New Guinea and had established a formidable base at Rabaul on New Britain. The missions flown by the handful of B-17s were more of a nuisance to the enemy than any real hindrance. The primary object was to delay the Japanese until American reinforcements could be brought to the Pacific.

The onslaught in the Pacific was turned back with a victory at the Battle of the Coral Sea on May 9, and then the American victory at Midway on June 7 put a new complexion on things. A new air commander arrived in the southwestern Pacific who would, through the years, lead the new Fifth Air Force to victory. His name was Gen. George Kenney. Reinforcements began to arrive via the 11th Bomb Group, and the 43rd Bomb Group was activated. At last a small stream of B-17Es began to arrive.

One of the more impressive missions against Rabaul was assembled and flown on August 7, 1942. A force of fifteen B-17s was slated for the mission. It would consist of nine Fortresses from the 93rd Bomb Squadron and six from the 28th and 30th Bomb Squadrons. The mission was under the command of Lt. Col. Richard Carmichael.

Numbers of aircraft from the 93rd Bomb Squadron gradually were depleted before the mission even began. One B-17 crashed on takeoff from Seven Mile drome base outside Port Moresby, New Guinea. Two more were forced to abort the mission with engine trouble shortly after takeoff. In the end, Maj. Felix Hardison led the mission with six 93rd Bomb Squadron B-17s. The "tail end Charlie" position was flown by Capt. Harl Pease, who had begged his way onto the mission, although the aircraft he was flying was plagued with electrical troubles and four engines that were long overdue for overhaul.

The bombers were forced to skirt some bad weather, but on arrival over Rabaul they found the target in the

Capt. (later Maj.) W. E. Chambers, pilot of The Aztec's Curse. *Chambers won two Silver Stars during the Guadalcanal campaign.* Chambers

Smoke rises from a target in the Solomons as The Aztec's Curse *returns from a mission.* Chambers

open. As they swept over the area from an altitude of 22,500ft they were attacked by some twenty Zero fighters. Despite the attack, the bombers continued to drop their loads while their gunners downed several enemy interceptors. In about 20 minutes the Fortresses made their way to cloud cover—except for the aircraft flown by Captain Pease, which had fallen behind the formation.

As it struggled along, Pease's aircraft had number two engine out. Then the flaming bomb-bay fuel tank dropped and the B-17 went down in flames with both inboard engines out and enemy fighters still swarming around their victim. The official report stated that the aircraft crashed in flames and that Captain Pease and crew were killed. For his exceptional gallantry in action, Captain Pease was post humously awarded the Medal of Honor.

Years later, it was determined that Captain Pease and his crewman, Sergeant Czechowski, had managed to parachute out of the flaming Fortress and had been taken prisoner by the Japanese. A Catholic priest who had

A Japanese warship under attack from B-17s during the Guadalcanal campaign. Chambers

31

A Japanese Zero comes in for attack on a B-17 during the Guadalcanal campaign. Chambers

American contemptuous humor illustrated by this nose art on a Pacific B-17. Giroux

been interned by the Japanese vividly remembered Pease and Czechowski who were in the prison camp with him until October 8, 1942. At that time, they were taken out for a so-called "work detail" and never seen again. Undoubtedly, they were executed by the enemy.

On August 7, 1942, the same day as the mission to Rabaul, US Marines landed on Guadalcanal in the Solomon Islands. B-17s that would support this campaign flew from an advanced base at Espiritu Santo in the New Hebrides chain. One of the Fortress pilots was a young Alabaman named Capt. W. E. Chambers of the 26th Bomb Squadron, 11th Bomb Group, who flew an aircraft named *The Aztec's Curse.*

Chambers flew one of his more successful missions on August 25. He reported: "Jap task force reported off Malaita Island . . . I led a flight of three. We arrived at point of contact and a Jap destroyer started shooting at us. We went a little farther and saw a large transport burning [it had been attacked by dive-bombers] and a cruiser moving in slowly to pick up survivors. Best target we could find, so made a run on him at 9,000ft, dropped 500lb bombs. Got three direct hits and several near misses. The explosions completely covered the ship. The crew was in an uproar, yelling back and forth on the intercom. No fighter opposition, thank goodness . . ."

Japanese records show that they lost the destroyer *Mitsuki* to B-17s on that day.

Chambers and crew would not be so lucky on the mission of October 4. By this time, the Fortresses frequently were using Guadalcanal as an advanced base. Chambers related: "The *Aztec Curse* took off at 0300 on a striking mission to Buka, flying number two position in a five-ship formation. The weather was pretty bad and flying night formation was hell. The flight hit a front just after daylight about fifty miles from the target and had to turn around. We flew right over two Japanese task forces, but the antiaircraft did no damage. Then we were attacked by twelve Zeros. They fell in line about 2,000ft above us and about five miles off to the left, between us and the sun, which had just come up, and peeled off one at a time. They came in from the front a little below us and then up, right through the formation. The first one came through and tried to half-roll back out, but misjudged his distance and crashed into the number five man in our formation. Both planes went down.

"The next one made the same attack, and I thought he was going to ram the lead ship. He just missed and stalled right over our formation on his back. All four of our ships were shooting at him and he was so close, I could see large pieces of metal and fabric coming off his engine and wings. As he fell, he started to burn. The pilot must have been dead because he had been firing all the time he came in and as he went down, I could still see lines of tracers coming from his guns.

"The rest came in, but did not attempt to come through the formation; they came in fast, took a quick shot, and then half-rolled out under the formation. The ball turrets got two more, one in flames and the other with one wing cut completely off. Number three ship had one engine shot out, but remained in formation. Two men jumped from the number five aircraft, but were machine gunned by the Zeros as they floated down. We landed at Cactus [Guadalcanal] at 0935. I don't think I have ever been so tired in my life."

Chambers flew another successful mission on October 15. Nine Fortresses took off from Espiritu Santo to attack Japanese troops landing on Guadalcanal. As Chambers recalled: "We found fourteen Japanese ships right in the harbor with four transports in near the shore landing troops. One transport had been torpedoed by a Navy PBY and was burning. Watched the second element make its run on a warship out in the bay. It scored several near misses and silenced some AA guns. I led my element around to the land side away from the ships and made a bombing run on one of the transports. Three Zeros attacked us while we were on the run, coming up underneath in frontal attacks and half-rolling away. Our ball turret gunner, Garvy, got the first one as he rolled out underneath us. The second one came in very close, so close I could see the flashes from all his guns and see tracers going into our right wing. As he rolled over on his back, Carter, our navigator, got in a good burst, and the whole plane seemed to burst into flames. During this time, Myers, our bombardier, dropped his bombs and the wingmen followed suit. We scored several hits and the

transport was burning as we headed home. As we hit the ground on landing, the plane started pulling to the right. The tire on that side had been hit and was flat . . . "

As Chambers continued his tour, he saw more and more of his fellow crews fall victim to the Japanese fighters. Soon the crews spent most of their time on Guadalcanal where their sleep was interrupted nightly by air raids, and all fell victim to malaria and dysentery. Still, they struck at Japanese shipping and bases day after day.

On one mission to Rabaul, the Fortresses ran into a storm so vicious that they had to fly on instruments for two and a half hours. As Chambers related: "I did a small amount of praying, and we finally broke out about fifty miles from the target. We arrived in the vicinity of Rabaul harbor, but could not find it on account of cloud cover and darkness. I started circling, waiting for daylight. All at once we were right in the middle of about forty searchlights, with AA bursting all over the place. I ducked in the clouds and lost them. I saw two large transports right together through a break in the clouds and made a run at 8,500ft. The AA was heavy, so I had to duck in a cloud before I could see the results of the two 1,000-pounders that Myers dropped . . . On the way back, I had

Gen. Douglas MacArthur's Flying Fortress, which was fitted out as a plush transport and aptly named Bataan. *Chambers*

to fly through the storm again . . . We broke out of the storm just before we reached the mountains, but arrived at our field to find it closed in and raining like hell. I had to land because of gas, so I came in over the field at 100ft downwind, made a 180 degree instrument turn, and made an instrument approach by compass. Was lucky and hit it right on the nose. Saw the ground 50ft above it and sat her down. Had ten minutes of gas left and I was worn out. I slept for a while, then went out and got skunk drunk."

After several months of flying missions under trying conditions, Chambers and his crew were finally relieved. As he summed it up at the time: "I think my combat flying is over. Out of fifty-four missions we have been on, we have flown *Curse* on at least forty-five. She has always gotten us back. There are sixteen crews out of thirty-eight left in the group and there is only one other crew that hasn't had a man injured. My crew is still intact and are the best bunch of fellows on earth. Our score stands at nine Zeros shot down, one cruiser sunk, two transports and one

Maj. Jay Zeamer (left) and Lt. Joseph R. Sarnoski (right) both won Medals of Honor on their mission to Buka in the Solomons on June 16, 1943. Despite serious wounds, they completed a vital photo-reconnaissance mission. USAAF

tanker sunk, and we had hits on other transports with the results unknown . . . The last time I saw the *Curse,* she was on Guadalcanal with her tail broken off. She's a grand ole lady and I wish I could bring her back to the States with us."

As time passed, the Fortresses in the Pacific were being replaced by Consolidated B-24 Liberators. Gen. Ira C. Eaker of the Eighth Air Force in England wanted the B-17s, and Gen. H. H. Arnold, commander of the Army Air Forces, agreed to give them to him.

One group that continued to fly the old Fortresses up to the bitter end in the Pacific was the 43rd Bomb Group. It was on one of their last B-17 missions that the action of two crewmen merited the Medal of Honor for both. On June 16, 1943, Capt. Jay Zeamer and his crew volunteered to fly a photo mission to Buka strip on Bougainville in the Solomon Islands. The crew was about ten miles from Buka when they were intercepted by about twenty Zeros. In the nose, bombardier Lt. Joseph R. Sarnoski downed the first attacking Zero while Sgt. John J. Able in the top turret took care of another. However, the Fortress had taken hits that disabled the oxygen system. Zeamer had to take the aircraft down from 28,000ft in a hurry.

As he pulled out of his dive, Zeamer's B-17 was attacked once more head-on. The Fortress pilot had gotten the armorers to install a fixed gun in the nose of the aircraft, which Zeamer could fire from a button on his yoke. As the Zero came in with guns blazing, Zeamer opened up and shot it down. At about the same time, the B-17 was hit in the nose with 20mm fire. Zeamer was wounded in the legs, so the copilot, Lt. John Britton, had to take over the rudder pedals.

The explosion of the 20mm shell had thrown Lieutenant Sarnoski back into the passageway under the flight deck, but Sarnoski called out that he was okay and went back to his gun. As another Zero came in, Sarnoski blazed away at it and then dropped to the floor, dead from a stomach wound.

The air battle raged for 40 minutes, during which time the Buka strip was photographed and five Zeros were downed by the crew. As the B-17 crew made their way back to base they were in dire circumstances. The pilot and copilot were both wounded, their radio was shot out and the operator wounded, and the top turret was still manned but the engineer was wounded. From time to time, Zeamer would pass out from loss of blood. Despite his wounds, engineer-gunner Sgt. John Able came down from his turret and stood behind the pilots and helped them fly the plane.

After almost three hours, the Fortress neared its destination. By this time, Sergeant Able had gotten the pilots to come around enough that they were able to land the aircraft with Lieutenant Britton on the rudder pedals and Captain Zeamer on the yoke. In their dazed condition they made a downwind landing, and with a crew of wounded men they were all fortunate to survive.

Zeamer and Sarnoski were both awarded the Medal of Honor, and each member of the crew was given the Distinguished Flying Cross.

By late 1943, just about all of the B-17s were gone from the Pacific and it became a theater of B-24 bombers. However, the B-17 had been there at the start and had done a tremendous job under appalling odds. From the very beginning, Boeing's Flying Fortress let the enemy know it had a most worthy opponent.

Chapter 4

England–The Daylight Bombing Experiment

America had stationed observers in England since the outbreak of World War II to report on the events transpiring in the conflict. Officers of the US Army Air Corps were on station during the Battle of Britain, and had followed closely the fortunes of the RAF's bombing campaign against Germany. When the United States entered the war following the attack on Pearl Harbor, the influx of American personnel in England was immediately stepped up, and planning began on what the mission of the Army Air Corps would be in the European Theater.

In February of 1942, General Eaker and a small staff went to England to prepare the groundwork for what would become the US Eighth Air Force. At that time the only thing they could accomplish was to negotiate for bases, set up logistic sites, and confer with RAF personnel regarding their operations and the associated facets that were necessary to begin bombing operations.

In April 1942, Gen. Carl "Tooey" Spaatz was appointed commander of American Air Forces in Europe, and he immediately requested that the new Eighth Air Force, which was in training in the southeastern United States, be assigned to England. His request was readily approved by Gen. H. H. Arnold, chief of staff of the US Army Air Forces, and the wheels of progress began to grind. Eighth Air Force headquarters was established at High Wycombe in Buckinghamshire, about thirty miles from London. Construction was begun on bases that would house the American units and in some cases, permanent RAF stations were slated to be turned over to the Americans.

The first unit selected for assignment to England was the 97th Bomb Group, which was training in Boeing B-17Es at Sarasota-Bradenton Airport in Florida. The unit was slated to get in 125 hours of flying time and 50 hours of instruction for ground echelon within six weeks. This was all being accomplished on a base that was still under construction and was sadly lacking in aircraft operations facilities. The 97th received overseas orders on May 12, 1942, and seven days later, the ground echelon boarded trains for their port of embarkation, Fort Dix, New Jersey.

The troops had a short stay at Fort Dix and boarded the former cruise liner *Queen Elizabeth* on the night of June 3. The unescorted ship made the trip in only six days and on June 9, the group boarded trains for their initial station in England at Polebrook.

The aircrews had to wait while the B-17s underwent engine changes and other modifications before they were ready for the flight over the Atlantic. By the last day of May the crews were at Presque Isle, Maine, awaiting their departure. Then their plans were changed: the Japanese bombed the Aleutian Islands in Alaska. The 97th Bomb Group plus the 1st Fighter Group, which had been scheduled to accompany the bombers overseas, were rushed to the West Coast. By the end of the month it had been decided that the attack on the Aleutians was a decoy to draw US forces away from Midway Island. The Fortresses of the 97th and the P-38s of the 1st Fighter Group headed back to Presque Isle.

Overseas movement of the air echelon began on June 26, and by July 27 the aircraft of the 97th were on station in England. Four aircraft were forced to land on the ice because of bad weather, but no personnel were lost.

From the beginning of planning for bomber operations over Europe, the RAF did its utmost to convince the Americans that daylight bombing would not be successful. They had tried it early in the war but were forced by heavy losses to switch to bombing under cover of darkness. They were satisfied with their night bombing program, and welcomed the Americans to join them in the nocturnal skies. Generals Spaatz and Eaker were both confirmed disciples of daylight precision bombing and felt that the American bombers were sufficiently armed and possessed capable performance to allow operations against targets on the Continent with reasonable losses. The Norden bombsight was de-

Fortresses lined up for takeoff on a mission over the Continent in the early days of daylight bombardment. USAAF

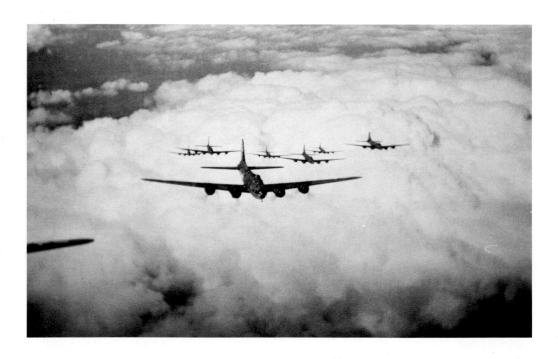

A Luftwaffe fighter pilot's view of a Fortress formation from his head-on attack position. USAAF

signed for pinpoint bombing, which was impossible at night, and failure to use such a weapon would be folly. Regardless of RAF objections, the Army Air Forces would have a go at daylight precision bombing.

Now that the 97th Bomb Group was on station, it was imperative that they be made ready for operations. This was difficult, however. The pilots had little instrument time, which was necessary in penetrating the English weather for assembly and letdown. And they had little experience flying formation, and tight formations were essential for their defense against Luftwaffe fighters. Navigators had no experience over Europe, and both navigators and radio operators needed to learn British communications procedures. The aerial gunners had no firing experience nor proper training for repelling enemy attack. The Luftwaffe fighters, however, and the antiaircraft batteries over the Continent were well trained and experienced. It was the greatest challenge that American aircrews ever faced.

August 17, 1942, marked the first mission by the B-17s of the Eighth Air Force. The target was the Sotteville marshaling yards in Rouen, one of the largest and busiest in France. Twelve Fortresses took off with Col. Frank Armstrong, commander of the 97th Bomb Group, and Maj. Paul Tibbetts in the lead aircraft. Gen. Ira Eaker was aboard the lead aircraft in the second flight, *Yankee Doodle,* which was flown by Lt. John P. Dowswell. A flight of six other B-17s was airborne to fly a diversionary route over the English Channel.

The first aircraft was airborne at 1526 hours and the formation sighted its first antiaircraft or flak over St. Valery. From an altitude of 23,000ft the bombers in vees of three dropped forty-five 600-pound bombs and nine 1,100-pounders. A few bombs hit about a mile short of the target, but the majority smashed into the assigned area. General Eaker reported, "A great pall of smoke and sand was left over the railroad tracks."

As the bombers turned off the target they encountered more flak and at Ypreville, the Luftwaffe put in an appearance where they were intercepted by the British Spitfire escorts. One Focke-Wulf Fw 190 made a turn into the formation where it received a burst from the ball

A B-17F is from the 401st Bomb Squadron, 91st Bomb Group. Mary Ruth *failed to return from a mission on June 22, 1943.* USAAF

turret guns of Sgt. Kent West. The Fortresses arrived home safely, with little damage.

The 97th was out again on August 19 when twenty-two B-17s bombed Abbeville Drucat airdrome in northern France. A number of aircraft were destroyed on the ground, and the airfield was put out of commission for a time while British commandos raided Dieppe. The next morning, RAF Spitfires escorted a dozen Fortresses to the Longureau marshaling yards, where they attacked an assemblage of 1,600

Fortresses from the 322nd Bomb Squadron, 91st Bomb Group over English cloud cover. Note the mottled paint. USAAF

A B-17F under attack from a Messerschmitt Bf 110, which can be seen at six o'clock high. USAAF

An Eighth Air Force Fortress streaming smoke from the number four engine nears a ditching position. Air-sea rescue saved many aircrew from the English Channel. USAAF

cars and seventeen engines. At least fifteen hits were scored on the target.

The first of many tragedies plagued the 97th when it flew to Rottendam on August 21. Twelve Fortresses took off, but four were forced to abort the mission because of mechanical troubles. The remaining aircraft were 16 minutes late for rendezvous with the escort fighters. When the formation reached the Dutch coast the bombers were recalled. The bombers' Spitfire escort soon had to depart, after which the bombers were attacked by twenty to twenty-five German fighters.

As a result of the fighter attacks, things were getting perilous in a Fortress named *Johnny Reb.* The tail gunner had gotten some hits, but in the top turret one of the guns had jammed. One of the waist gunners had a blob of ice in his mask and was trying to fire his gun with one hand and clear the mask with the other. In the nose, the navigator had fired at a crossing fighter when a burst of cannon fire tore through the windshield on the flight deck. Copilot Lt. Donald A. Walter was fatally wounded and pilot Lt. Richard S. Starks suffered from plexiglass splinters. As he struggled for breath, Lieutenant Starks managed to call for help and got bombardier Lt. Edward Sconiers and engineer-gunner Sergeant Allen to come up and assist.

Lieutenant Sconiers managed to get the dead copilot out of his seat, and replaced him at the controls. The pilot instructed Sconiers, while Sergeant Allen did his best to aid the wounded men. The Fortress dropped out of formation, but managed to make it home safely despite the loss of two engines.

On September 6, the 301st Bomb Group flew its first mission when it accompanied the 97th back to the Sotteville marshaling yards. The following day, the 92nd Bomb Group joined in and the Fortresses took their first losses. The Luftwaffe fighters initiated their deadly head-on attacks on the B-17s by sections and downed two of them—one from the 92nd Group and one from the 97th. The 97th also brought home one dead gunner and three wounded crew members.

October 9 marked a historic point for VIII Bomber Command. The 306th Bomb Group flew its first mission, and the Fortresses were joined by the 93rd Bomb Group in B-24s to mark the first time more than 100 American bombers joined in operations. However, this would mark the last mission of the 92nd Bomb Group for some months, as they would become a training unit for incoming bomber crews.

October 21 proved to be the 97th Bomb Group's final mission with the 8th Air Force (the group would depart for North Africa in early November to support the American invasion there) when the 97th, 301st, and 306th Bomb Groups took off to bomb the submarine pens at Lorient, France. The 301st and 306th returned early, however, because of solid overcast over the English Channel. The 97th Group plowed on and broke out over the target at 17,500ft. The enemy was taken by surprise, and the Fortresses let go thirty 2,000lb bombs of which twenty-one hit within 1,000ft of the target. Workshops and floating docks were destroyed, but the bombs failed to penetrate the submarine shelters' thick cement covering.

As the B-17s turned off the target they were attacked by thirty-six German fighters. First hit was the Fortress of Lt. Francis X. Schwarzenbeck. As the B-17 went down, the crew continued to blaze away at the enemy fighters when they should have been bailing out. Two enemy fighters were seen to fall to their guns. The bombardier and three gunners survived. Two other Fortress crews were lost in the fight. The mission to Lorient marked the heaviest loss to any bomber group to date.

Missions continued against the U-boat installations along the French coast through October and into November. The 301st Group flew its last mission from England on November 8, and then departed for North Africa. This left the 8th Air Force with only the 306th and the 91st Bomb Groups, the latter of which had flown its first mission the previous day. These two groups would be joined by the 303rd and 305th Bomb Groups on November 17. These four B-17 units would carry the load until May 1943.

A mission to St. Nazaire, France, on November 23 brought about a sharp fight with the Luftwaffe, and one crew set quite a record as they were singled out by Fw 190s from Jagdgeschwader 2 (JG 2). The targeted Fortress was the 306th Group's *Banshee* and was flown by Lt. William J. Casey. In a 12 minute

Hell's Angels *from the 303rd Bomb Group was the first B-17 to complete twenty-five missions.* USAAF

Fortresses of the 96th Bomb Group beginning to leave contrails over a spotty undercast. USAAF

S/Sgt. Maynard "Snuffy" Smith receives his Medal of Honor from Secretary of War Henry Stimson. USAAF

running fight with the Focke-Wulfs, his crew downed seven enemy fighters. As noted by the 306th historian, "Parley D. Small, the tail gunner, got the first at 1328 hours at 400 yards with the pilot bailing out.

"Waist Gunner Reginald Harris hit one at 200 yards at 1334; the plane went

into the water with no escape for the pilot.

"Joe Bowles in the ball turret scored at 1335, destroying the attacker at 50 yards as the plane broke into flames.

"Engineer Wilson Elliott caught one at two o'clock high and saw it disintegrate in the air at 200 yards.

"At 1338 Harris got his second at 100 yards; the pilot bailed out.

"Bowles hit his second, catching the fighter as it zoomed towards his ball turret. He used only 70 rounds of ammuni-

tion and watched the plane hit the water.

"Allan Meaux in the waist got his at 1340; the plane fell out of control and plunged into the sea."

Lieutenants A. G. Smith, bombardier, and Walter Leeker, navigator, were both wounded, but Casey managed to bring them all home intact.

The mission to Romilly-Sur-Seine on December 20, 1942, really stirred up the Luftwaffe. They rose in great numbers on the route in and even more so on the route out. One crew that was heavily involved in the fight was that of Lt. Bruce Barton of the 91st Bomb Group, who was flying a B-17 named *Chief Sly.* He was flying the right wing of Capt. Ken Wallick, who was leading the strike against the airdrome south of Paris, one of the deepest penetrations the bombers had made.

The weather was beautiful, and the bombers assembled and headed out for the target with great expectations. Soon after they crossed the Channel, however, they ran into fighters. Barton stated: "Focke-Wulf 190s—world of them. I watched them circle around and make their attacks, but never did get worked up because they didn't seem to be shooting at me. I guess my crew was a bit excited, for they had never seen so many fighters. The pressure was lifted when they all agreed over the intercom that one of the waist gunners had shot down a fighter . . ."

The Fortresses of the 91st Bomb Group went over the target where there was little flak and made a good bomb run. The group had lost two B-17s in the fight inbound, but now the enemy had disappeared, the formation was good, and visibility was excellent. About this time, the fighters returned.

As Barton saw it: "Yes, they were out to our right. The sky was black with them. Then they began their attacks. It seemed as though they were all coming in off our right wing. One behind the other they came—all shooting. At first I thought they were all coming straight for us, but they broke and picked on the group below and ahead of us. That group really caught hell. The fighters were flying right through the formation, shooting everything they had. I sat up above and watched it as though I was in the balcony of a theater seeing a movie. Two fighters went down flaming; a B-17 ex-

ploded in mid-air; another dropped behind on fire and parachutes began to pop out of it. It was a great show, but it left a sunken feeling inside of me.

"Then they started on us! I was too busy flying a tight formation to see much of what was going on. It seemed as though every gun on our ship was firing all the time. I glanced over once to see a Focke-Wulf break away only a few feet off our right wing tip. It had a big yellow nose and I could see the pilot sitting there. I turned back and stuck my wing closer into my leader as we held a mean formation. The gunners were clocking fighters in from everywhere and occasionally they would report one going down.

"I saw one coming in straight ahead underneath and called for the ball turret man, S/Sgt. Myron Srsen, to get him. He

got him all right, for I watched the tracers going straight into the cockpit. Then the plane burst into flames. I couldn't watch the fighters while flying, so I let my copilot, Lt. Arthur Reynolds, watch out for them. Several times he grabbed the yoke and pushed it down quickly as the bullets of the enemy passed over our heads.

"We only got a few scattered holes out of the fray, but the worst was yet to come. Wallick's lead ship got hit badly. One of the engines was burning, and the plane was vibrating badly. He couldn't stay in formation under such conditions, so he gradually began to drop behind and down. I saw nothing to do but stay on his wing and give him as much protection as possible . . . "

Barton continued: "I could see the English Channel in front of us as we be-

Capt. Robert K. Morgan and the crew of Memphis Belle *are congratulated on the completion of their combat tour. They were the first Eighth Air Force crew to do so.* USAAF

gan to get hit. The attacks were still coming from the right so we got the worst of it. First it was holes in the wings and scattered holes in the fuselage. The tail gunner was hit in the face as a 20mm shell burst in front of him. Then bullets ripped into our number three engine and we lost it entirely. Then number four engine started smoking from a hole in the oil line.

"I was still in formation with Wallick when something hit the tail knocking a hole three feet wide and eight feet long—which threw us tumbling out of formation. It took the strength of both of

41

This photograph shows the defensive formation that was used by the Eighth Air Force on its combat missions. USAAF

us in the cockpit to pull the vibrating plane out of the dive. Just then another burst caught us in the right wing, cutting the aileron control loose and jamming the aileron in the up position, tending to pull us to the right into our dead engines. We let one fighter slide in from above, which almost got us. His bullets raked across the cockpit and top turret. They missed me by inches and Reynolds said, 'They got Hare.' Technical Sergeant Hare, our top turret gunner, looked like he had been hit, for we saw his knees bending. Actually, he was not hit, only tailing the plane overhead with his guns, this bending his knees. He had had a close call . . . Shortly thereafter he ran out of ammunition, but continued to operate the turret so the fighters around us wouldn't know he was through."

Barton sighted some clouds several thousand feet below and headed for them, but six Fw 190s accompanied him. Barton added, "I had always heard that in such a case one should turn into the attacks. I think the hardest thing I ever had to do in my life was to make myself turn the battered plane into the fighters that were headed toward us. I closed my eyes, hoping it would work. And it did. They missed with their shots. After that, it was easier to evade their attacks."

As Barton neared the clouds, he straightened out. That was a mistake; another fighter was able to make a pass and his bullets shattered the nose of the aircraft and wounded the navigator, Lt. Paul Burnett, in the leg. Limping along, Barton managed to make England and bring his battered Fortress down in a cabbage patch.

It was during this period that a man whose name would become synonymous with strategic bombing came to the forefront. The man was Col. Curtis LeMay, commander of the 305th Bomb Group. He was a veteran B-17 pilot from the early days at Langley Field, Virginia, and perhaps no one knew the capability of the aircraft more than he. The first

Yes, pets were very important to Eighth Air Force crew members. Here, Capt. Warren Cerrone and his dog Jeff. C. B. Rollins

change that he inaugurated in his unit was the formation. He favored a system whereby two or three squadrons flew in a stepped-up formation of eighteen aircraft. These aircraft were staggered into three-plane elements within the group to form a box formation, thus giving aircraft mutual protection support and forming up well for pattern bombing.

The second thing that LeMay did was to eliminate evasive action on the bomb run. Bombing results from the early missions largely had been poor. LeMay knew the major reason for this was that most of the aircraft were using evasive action to evade enemy flak right up to the final seconds before the bombs were dropped. He sat down and calculated from an old artillery manual the rate of fire, distance, and so on, and found that the odds against being hit at bombing altitudes were favorable. From that day on, the Fortresses in LeMay's unit flew straight and level from the initial point through the bomb run, regardless of the time elapsed. This theory caused much unrest with the crews, however, and many felt that to follow LeMay's orders would be suicide.

The test came on January 3, 1943, when LeMay led his 305th Bomb Group against St. Nazaire. They used their staggered formation and held straight and steady on the bomb run. The group suffered no losses during the 9 minutes before bombs away. The bombing was effective, and it also proved that an excellent pattern could be covered using the lead bombardier method whereby all other bombardiers dropped their bombs

when the lead aircraft did. It would be only a short time before the other groups in the 8th Air Force adopted LeMay's tactics.

January 27, 1943, marked the first mission of 8th Air Force heavy bombers against Germany. The target was the naval base at Wilhelmshaven. Four groups of B-17s were dispatched to the

This ball turret took a direct hit right in the view plate. USAAF

target, and fifty-five dropped their loads. Only one Fortress was lost, even though the Luftwaffe put up every type of fighter they had available. The Battle of Germany had begun!

Chapter 5

Air Battles over the Reich

The initial mission against Germany proper brought a new complexion to the air war over Europe. With the buildup of American bomber forces in England, the Luftwaffe came under tremendous pressure not only from Air Marshal Hermann Goering, but also from Adolf

Lt. William R. Lawley, who won the Medal of Honor by bringing his wounded crewmen home on February 20, 1944. USAAF

Hitler to protect the Fatherland from bombardment. Reinforcements were brought in for the fighter forces in the West, and tactics were developed to combat the bomber formations. The year 1943 would find the bomber formations of the Eighth Air Force fighting not only to complete their missions and to prove daylight bombing a success, but before it was over, the crews themselves would be fighting for their very existence.

Up to this point, the majority of B-17s used by the 8th Air Force were F models, which were very similar to the early E models. The main visible changes were the new plexiglass nose and the paddle-blade propellers. Many other changes had been made, however, including new electrical and oxygen systems and a new and more powerful Wright R-1820 engine that developed 1,380hp under emergency conditions. Many of the new modified F models were fitted with the new "Tokyo tank" fuel cells in the outer wing sections.

Additionally, a number of field modifications were made. With the head-on attacks by German fighters, which had been initiated by Luftwaffe ace Oberst Egon Meyer of Luftwaffe fighter group II/JG 2, the lack of nose armament had become apparent. Many of the bomb groups had come up with various modifications in the plexiglass nose where two guns could be fitted, while others had fitted the nose section with "cheek"

guns. Later F-model B-17s were fitted with cheek gun positions at the factory.

The crews also suffered from the extreme cold at high altitudes over northwestern Europe. The outside temperature at 25,000ft was often 40–50 degrees below zero Fahrenheit. The open waist windows sent sweeping frigid air across the gunners, and back to the tail position. The gunners in the rear of the aircraft nearly froze. The radio operator, with an open hatch above his position, fared no better. The first baby blue electrically heated suits may not have been perfect, but they were a real godsend to all crew members. The other great innovation was the introduction of flak suits. These vest-like protectors contained quilted steel plates that were effective against shrapnel and fragments from explosive 20mm fire. The flak suits were supplemented by steel helmets with steel earflaps that were worn particularly while the aircraft was on a bomb run. Later, the gunners were blessed with the installation of plexiglass waist windows and plexiglass radio-room hatches.

As losses began to mount among bomber crews, the men began to bemoan their fates. How many missions would they be subjected to before they would be relieved from combat? As their numbers began to dwindle, it didn't take a genius to figure that the odds were against *any* of them making it, even when the combat tour was set at twenty-five missions. As the air war continued over Germany and US losses rose, the morale sunk even further. But early in 1943 more hope and determination existed among the troops.

On February 4, 1943, the bombers were slated to strike at Hamm, Germany, but weather prevented it, so Emden was struck as a secondary target by some of the Fortress groups. The Luftwaffe was up in strength, and for the first time, twin-engine fighters made their appearance. Five Fortresses were lost, one of them colliding with a Focke-Wulf 190.

This mission was significant for one crew of the 91st Bomb Group. The crew of Lt. William J. Crumm, which flew *Jack the Ripper,* completed their eleventh and final mission that day. They had been selected to return to the United States and instruct new units in the operations of the 8th Air Force bombers. Upon their return, they wrote a manual that would serve as an invaluable tool for crews who would be going to England to join in the fight over northwestern Europe.

On March 4, 1943, four groups of B-17s set out to bomb the marshaling yards at Hamm, in the industrial Ruhr region of Germany. After they formed up and headed out on course for the target, they encountered heavy clouds. The Fortresses plowed on toward the target. As conditions grew worse, all but one of the groups turned back for England: The 91st Bomb Group continued eastward. The lead navigator reported that they had crossed the coast and then the weather broke and the skies were clear. With sixteen B-17s still in formation Maj. Paul Fishburne chose to continue on to the target.

The Fortresses of the 91st put eighty 1,000lb bombs on the target, but in the course of the mission, they encountered a Luftwaffe force of over one hundred fighters. The enemy pilots swarmed around the B-17s like bees and pressed their attacks in so close that the Fortress crew could see their faces. Four bombers fell to Luftwaffe guns, while several others barely made it home.

The most notable survival story was that of Capt. George Birdsong and his crew. They were so determined to make the mission, they had rushed back to their base and loaded up in another aircraft named *Stormy Weather* when their

A Fortress comes off a target that is still in the process of trying to cover itself with a smoke screen. USAAF

"Bombs away" from Devil's Daughter *of the 95th Bomb Group.* USAAF

306th Bomb Group Fortresses wound up and ready to go. Loaded down, this was always a moment of truth. 306th BG Assn.

A most unusual tiger tail design on a Fortress from the 306th Bomb Group. 306th BG Assn.

own aircraft had engine trouble while forming up for the strike. They were hit by German fighters before they got to the target and on the initial attack, the oxygen tank under the pilot's seat was hit and knocked out. This started a fire which top turret gunner T/Sgt. Eugene Remmel and navigator Lt. Ernie Miller managed to get under control. Yet, the flight deck was still so full of smoke that Birdsong couldn't even see his copilot next to him.

Captain Birdsong's aircraft made the bomb run. The bombardier called, "Bombs away," not knowing that the bomb bay doors had not opened. As they came off target, one of the German fighters hit them with 20mm fire. Number two engine was hit by one shell, then Lieutenant Miller was painfully wounded by the second, and a third shell came through the cockpit windshield, seriously wounding the copilot and sending a glass fragment into Birdsong's eye.

Sergeant Rummel managed to lift the copilot off the controls and carry him to the radio room for first aid. Then another fighter attack came and knocked out number three engine. Birdsong had both surviving engines at full throttle while trying to see through the blood flowing down his face. *Stormy Weather* lagged behind, but managed to stay with

The B-17 Little Audrey *flew with the 306th Bomb Group. 306th BG Assn.*

the formation out over the North Sea. As they crossed the water, the crew discovered that they still had their bombs aboard. Then they had to reinstall the safety pins, for the Fortress had let down too low for the bombs to be salvoed.

Birdsong brought the B-17s in to Bassingborn only to discover that the brakes were inoperable. The aircraft went off the end of the runway, through a fence, across a road, and then through a field of Brussels sprouts. At this point, the crew jumped out of the aircraft, bringing their wounded with them. Torn and bloodied, they had made it home!

For their successful lone strike against Hamm, the 91st Bomb Group was awarded a Distinguished Unit Citation.

It was on a mission to Vegesack, Germany, to bomb U-boat yards on March 18 that a member of VIII Bomber Command would win the command's first Medal of Honor. Lt. Jack Mathis was a bombardier in the 303rd Bomb Group aboard a B-17 named *The Duchess*. While the aircraft was on the bomb run it was hit by flak, but as the navigator noted, Mathis didn't seem to pay any attention to the interruption. He stayed at his bombsight and called out, "Bomb bay doors open."

The navigator related: "On the bomb run, flak hit us. We were seconds short of the bomb release point when a whole barrage of flak hit our squadron, which we were leading. One of the shells burst out to the right and a little below the nose. It couldn't have been over 30ft away when it burst. If it had been much closer it would have knocked the whole plane over.

"A hunk of flak came tearing through the side of the nose. It shattered the glass on the right side and broke through with a loud crash. I saw Jack falling back toward me and threw up my arm to ward off the fall. By that time, both of us were back in the rear of the nose—blown back there I guess, by flak burst. I was sort of half standing, half lying against the back wall and Jack was leaning up against me. I didn't know he was injured at the time.

"Without any assistance from me, he pulled himself back to his bombsight. His little seat had been knocked out from under him by flak and he sort of knelt over the bombsight. He knew that as bombardier of the lead ship, the re-

Raunchy Wolf *was a B-17F from the 551st Squadron, 385th Bomb Group.* USAAF

The B-17F Liberty Belle, *serial number 42-30096, flew with the 544th Squadron, 385th Bomb Group.* USAAF

Hoosier Hot Shot, *B-17G serial number 42-38006, flew with the 91st Bomb Group, Eighth Air Force.* USAAF

Another 91st Bomb Group B-17G, Pist'l Packin' Mama. USAAF

The B-17 Betty Lou's Buggy *of the Eighth Air Force's 91st Bomb Group.* USAAF

sults of the whole squadron might depend on his accuracy. And he didn't let anything stop him. Part of my job as navigator is to keep the log of the flights, so I looked at my watch to start timing the fall of the bombs. I heard Jack call out on the intercom, 'Bombs . . .' He usually called it out in sort of a singsong. But he never finished the phrase this time.

"I looked up and saw Jack reaching over to grasp the bomb bay door handle to close the doors. Just as he pushed the handle, he slumped over backwards. I caught him. That was the first indication that anything was wrong. I saw that his arm was pretty badly shot. 'I guess they got you this time old boy,' I remember saying, but then his head slumped over and I saw that the injuries were more serious than just some flak in the arm. I knew then that he was dead. I closed the bomb bay and returned to my post."

Lt. Jack Mathis had made the supreme effort to get back to his bombsight in order to enable his squadron to put their bombs on target.

April 17 marked the fiercest opposition that the Fortress crews had experienced to date. One hundred fifteen B-17s from four bomb groups were dispatched to strike the Focke-Wulf 190 plant at Bremen, Germany. With the 91st Bomb Group leading, the bombers began to encounter enemy fighters just past the Frisian Islands. The fighter attacks were coordinated, with head-on attacks against four to six enemy aircraft at a time. They went after the bombers throughout the route in, and even attacked through the flak over the target. It was reported that Junkers Ju 88 twin-engine aircraft dropped some sort of aerial bombs on the B-17 formations from above. Bombing results were reported as being good, but sixteen aircraft were lost out of the leading combat formation. The 91st Bomb Group lost six aircraft, while the 306th Bomb Group lost ten.

In addition to the fighter attacks, the 306th Bomb Group reported they encountered the heaviest concentration of flak they had ever seen. The Eighth Air Force flak officer's report stated: "The intensity of the flak was probably the most severe that has ever been experienced by this wing, and the huge volume of smoke that overhung the target area acted as a very real deterrent, causing many members of crews to feel that it would be an impossibility to fly in the area without suffering damage."

Capt. William J. Casey, leading the 367th Bomb Squadron of the 306th Bomb Group, had his aircraft *Banshee* raked over by fighters and his crew fought valiantly, but the deteriorating condition of the aircraft forced Casey to head his plane back to land as his one remaining engine was running away. During the repeated fighter attacks and the final pass by a twin-engine fighter, the five crewmen in the back of the bomb bay were all killed. At 23,000ft the men up front began leaving the plane, planning to open their chutes immediately so that the high winds aloft might blow them over land in the Frisian Islands. All made it, although they landed close to water and were captured almost immediately.

Lt. Maxwell Judas, the only 368th Bomb Squadron plane to make it home, was hit hard on the bomb run by fighters and as he turned off the target, all of his squadron disappeared. Unable to maintain altitude, Judas was forced to descend to 500ft. He nursed his aircraft back across the North Sea with about an engine and a half, flying all the way to Thurleigh at 105mph indicated airspeed.

In *Old Faithful*, Capt. Pervis Youree traveled down the bomb run with two engines feathered and the top turret shattered after encountering a Luft-

Fickle Finger of ? *was B-17F serial number 42-3335 of the 385th Bomb Group, Eighth Air Force.* USAAF

The Vibrant Virgin, *a B-17F, serial number 42-30275, was assigned to the 548th Bomb Squadron, 385th Bomb Group.* USAAF

Stars and Stripes, 2nd Edition *was a B-17G assigned to the Eighth Air Force's 385th Bomb Group.* USAAF

waffe welcome. Youree also had to take his plane down on the deck, and flew 200 miles at wave-top heights with one engine. Lt. Leroy Sugg, the copilot, held together the control cables for the number three engine with his hands. With full power on one engine, Youree was able to make 115mph indicated airspeed. The crew busily jettisoned everything, including the ball turret.

The 306th Bomb Group mission report by Maj. John L. Lambert included the following: "On the way in from the coast some forty E/A in string formation flew parallel to our formation, level and about 2,000 yards to the left. Attacks were withheld until we were on the bombing run, when there were heavy attacks . . . The 306th Group fell out of column to the left, with resulting concentrated head-on attacks . . . Dozens of E/A sailed right into and through our formation, rolling over and diving as they passed through. This was the period when heaviest losses were sustained."

A mission to the U-boat pens at St. Nazaire, France, marked the second event that would bring a Medal of Honor to a B-17 crew member. Sgt. Maynard

H. "Snuffy" Smith was flying his first mission as a crew member assigned to the ball turret. The aircraft belonged to the 306th Bomb Group and was flown by Lt. L. P. Johnson. As the Fortress came off the target and headed for home it was hit by fighters, causing serious destruction and setting fires in the aircraft.

Smith related the events from that moment: "My interphone and the electrical controls to my turret went out, so I hand-cranked myself up and crawled out of the turret into the ship. The first thing I saw was a sheet of flame coming out of the radio room and another fire by the tail wheel section.

"Suddenly the radio operator came staggering out of the flames. He made a beeline for the gun hatch and dove out. I glanced out and watched him hit the horizontal stabilizer, bounce off, and open his chute. By this time the right waist gunner had bailed out over his gun and the left waist gunner was trying to jump, but was stuck half in and half out of his gun hatch. I pulled him back into the ship and asked him if the heat was too much for him. All he did was stare at me and I watched him bail out the rear door. His chute opened okay.

"The smoke and gas were really thick. I wrapped a sweater around my face so I could breathe, grabbed a fire ex-

tinguisher, and attacked the fire in the radio room. Glancing over my shoulder at the tail fire, I thought I saw something coming and ran back. It was Gibson, the tail gunner, painfully crawling back, wounded. He had blood all over him.

"Looking him over, I saw that he had been hit in the back and that it had probably gone through his left lung. I laid him down on his left side so that the wound would not drain into the right lung, gave a shot of morphine, and made him as comfortable as possible before going back to the fires.

"I had just got started in this when this Fw 190 came in again. I jumped for one of the waist guns and fired at him. As he swept under us I turned to the other waist gun and let him have it from the other side. He left us for a while so I went back to the radio room fire again.

"I got into the room this time and began throwing out burning debris. The fire had burned holes so large in the side of the ship that I had just tossed the stuff out through them. Gas from a burning extinguisher was choking me, so I went back to the tail fire. I took off my chute so I could move easier. I'm glad I didn't take it off sooner, because later I found that it had stopped a .30 caliber bullet.

"I fired another burst with the waist guns and went back to the radio room with the last of the extinguisher fluid. When that ran out I found a water bottle and a urine can and poured these out.

"After that I was so mad, I urinated on the fire and finally beat on it with my hands and feet until my clothes began to smolder. That Fw 190 came around again and I let him have it. That time he left us for good. The fire was under control, more or less, and we were in sight of land."

Johnson brought the aircraft in for a landing at Predonnock but as he let the tail wheel down and slowed, the fuselage began to crack at the trailing edge of the wing and finally crumpled to a standstill.

Another amazing B-17 survival story took place on May 15 in a Fortress named *Old Bill* that belonged to the 305th Bomb Group. The Fortresses had taken off to bomb Wilhelmshaven but when the target was found not to be visible, the formation headed for Heligoland on the coast. *Old Bill* was flown

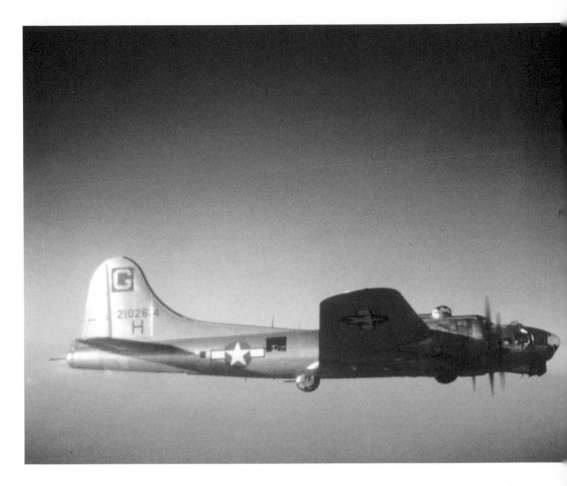

by Capt. William D. Whitson, along with his regular crew, who had brought the aircraft overseas with the original contingent.

Enemy aircraft were encountered, and on one of the first passes, the oxygen system was shot out. Whitson had no choice but to dive the aircraft down from 25,000ft to an altitude where the crew could breathe. Not only had they lost their oxygen, but Whitson had been wounded in the leg.

Whitson went to the rear to check for damage and get some portable oxygen bottles. When he returned to the flight deck he found his copilot, Lt. Harry L. Holt, almost unconscious for lack of oxygen. Once Holt was revived, Whitson returned to the rear to have his wounds treated.

Shortly after Whitson returned, the aircraft was attacked by some twenty German fighters. As the Focke-Wulf 190s made their head-on passes they shot through the cockpit windshield, seriously wounding Holt and hitting Whitson for the second time.

The plexiglass nose was completely shot away and navigator Lt. Douglas Venable had been killed. The bombardier saved his own life by throwing himself flat when he saw the German fighters blazing in at his level.

Shell fragments had splintered the top turret and wounded engineer-gunner T/Sgt. Albert Haymon in the head. Although blood streamed down, Haymon operated the turret and guns with an emergency hand-crank until the crank jammed.

The tail gunner, T/Sgt. Kenneth Meyer, was firing away at the enemy fighters with vigor. He claimed three destroyed in rapid order. In the ball turret, S/Sgt. Edgar Nichols kept firing despite his wounds, and hit two fighters. Right waist gunner Sgt. John Breen downed another.

Once the top turret was no longer operative, Sergeant Haymon left it to as-

Formation view from the tail gunner's seat. Copilots on the lead aircraft often took this position to report on the unit's formation. C. B. Rollins

Madam Shoo Shoo *was one of the attractive nose art girls that flew with the 385th Bomb Group.* C. B. Rollins

Pfc. Ruby Newell was elected the most attractive WAC in England, and this 385th Bomb Group aircraft was named after her. C. B. Rollins

sist radio operator T/Sgt. Fred Brewak in moving Lieutenant Holt back to the radio room. Then Haymon went forward again and took over the copilot's seat.

Sergeant Meyer ran out of ammunition and went up to the waist for more. When it was expended, he returned to the waist and manned one of the guns there until the fighter attacks ceased. At that time, Meyer went up and replaced Haymon in the copilot's seat.

Although he was wounded, bombardier Lieutenant Barrall went up to the flight deck where he helped Captain Whitson with his wounds and gave him a shot of morphine for the pain. He then returned to the nose. Despite the tremendous blast of air through the missing plexiglass, Barrall manned the cheek gun and managed to put telling shots into a Messerschmitt Bf 210 that came to finish off *Old Bill.* Following this encounter, Barrall went back to the flight deck and took over the controls in the copilot's position.

The rear of the aircraft was a mess. Bullet and flak holes had riddled the interior. Of the eleven men who were aboard *Old Bill* only two had not been wounded, Sergeant Meyer and right waist gunner Sergeant Breen. Overall, the balance of *Old Bill* was not good. The right wing was buckled and its hydraulics were shot out. Regardless, Whitson brought the Fortress in for a successful, wheels-down landing at its home base at Chelveston.

On examining the shot-up bomber on the ground, the group flight surgeon was heard to say, "Not a damn thing in there but blood and empty cartridge cases."

For their outstanding action that day, the crew of *Old Bill* became the most decorated aviators of the 303rd Bomb Group. Captain Whitson and Lieutenant Barrall each received the Distinguished Service Cross, and other crew members received eight Silver Stars and seven Purple Hearts.

May 17, 1943, was a triumphant day for Capt. Robert K. Morgan and several of his crew members of the 91st Bomb Group. They became the first Eighth Air Force bomber crew to complete a tour of twenty-five combat missions. Flying in their Fortress *Memphis Belle,* they had beaten the odds and now they were slated to return to the United States for a War Bond Tour. From there,

Fortresses of the 95th Bomb Group en route to a target in Norway. USAAF

they would visit various bases where new crews were being trained for combat in the Eighth Air Force.

The *Memphis Belle* had completed only twenty-four missions on May 17 when its skipper and several other crew members finished up their tour, so it was up to another pilot to see the valiant craft through its twenty-fifth mission. The honor went to Lt. C. L. Anderson and crew, who took the *Memphis Belle* to Kiel on May 19, 1943. Although *Belle* was not the first to complete a tour, the bomber would receive the lion's share of publicity for the feat on its return to the United States. The honor of being the first B-17 to complete twenty-five missions went to *Hell's Angels* of the 303rd Bomb Group, which returned from its twenty-fifth on May 14, 1943.

On May 27, 1943, the 8th Air Force introduced a new weapon when it struck at the submarine pens at St. Nazaire. The new aircraft was the Boeing YB-40, a heavily armed version of the B-17. The new Fortress was armed with the conventional top turret, ball turret, and tail guns, but there were several new additions. A Martin twin-gun power turret was installed in the radio room, each waist installation was fitted with twin .50 caliber guns that were hydraulically boosted, and a chin turret with twin .50s was installed under the plexiglass nose. The latter turret would become standard on B-17Gs in late 1943. The aircraft arrived without the cheek guns in the nose but these were installed before combat, bringing the total number of .50 caliber guns aboard to sixteen. The ad-

vised total ammunition load was 11,200 rounds. The additional guns and ammunition brought the total weight of the YB-40 at takeoff to some 10,000lb more than a loaded B-17F.

A dozen of the YB-40s were assigned to the 92nd Bomb Group and would fly not only with the 92nd, but on occasion would be used by other bomb groups in their formation. From its first mission to St. Nazaire, the aircraft was not a success. The plane carried no bomb load, so when the B-17s in the formation dropped their bombs, the YB-40s—still laden with heavy guns and ammunition—could not keep up. Ammunition feed re-

A 385th Bomb Group comes home to roost. Operations officers are out by the flight control trailer to check in the birds. C. B. Rollins

An olive drab Fortress teams up with a shiny new silver sister aircraft from the 306th Bomb Group. 306th BG Assn.

quired modification. Although the aircraft was tested under various conditions, the only real advantage that it brought about was the chin turret. By July of 1943, the YB-40 would be history.

A mission to Kiel on June 13, 1943, proved to be disastrous for the 4th Bomb Wing which was composed of the 94th, 95th, and 96th Bomb Groups. The 95th would suffer its highest loss of the war when ten of its Fortresses fell, and the 94th would lose nine. The 96th was fortunate to get out with only three losses. All total, twenty-two aircraft in sixty attacks were lost, or about 30 percent.

The wing was led by Brig. Gen. Nathan Bedford Forrest, grandson of the famed Civil War Confederate Cavalry general, who had come direct from Washington to take over a combat wing. Rather than fly the staggered formation that had been adopted by the other 8th Air Force bombers, the 4th would fly a flat, wingtip-to-wingtip formation over the target, as decreed by General Forrest. The general also had instructed that the gunners use a new type of oil for their guns which supposedly would prevent their freezing.

General Forrest flew in the copilot's seat of the lead aircraft with Capt. Harry Stirwalt as pilot. The formation moved across the North Sea and then began to make its penetration toward the Kiel shipyards. At that moment, hordes of enemy fighters began to appear. The Bf 109s and Fw 190s came in waves from head-on and did their utmost to close to the point that they could break up the formation.

As the Fortresses made their bomb run, the attacks continued. One after another, B-17s began to fall. The aircraft on which General Forrest was flying dropped its bombs and then went down. Only two men survived of the thirteen men aboard; General Forrest was not one of them.

A number of B-17s went down because many of their guns were frozen. It was not unusual for half the guns of one of the 95th Bomb Group's aircraft to be unserviceable because of the new type oil that had been used. Those who *could* fire did their utmost to turn back the Luftwaffe fighters. As the Fortresses fought their way over the North Sea they dropped down to about 800ft, but still were attacked over and over by Luftwaffe pilots. One German fighter collided with one of the B-17s which in turn collided with another B-17. All three aircraft crashed into the sea. In addition to the ten aircraft lost on the mission, the 95th Group had one B-17 crash-land upon reaching England.

To the crews of the 94th Bomb Group, the attacks of the German fighters seemed suicidal. Pilots reported that they had to take violent evasive action to keep some of the fighters from crashing into them. The group came under especially heavy attack as they rallied off the target. Six of their nine aircraft losses came in the target area. Maj. Louis Thorup managed to get his shot-up Fortress over the North Sea with one engine out. There he was attacked by a flight of four Bf 109s, one of which made a pass that knocked out another two engines and shot off the entire left stabilizer. Thorup managed to stay aloft a few more miles and set the plane down in the sea. Fortunately, the crew was rescued eleven hours later.

The final analysis of the mission was that the abandonment of the staggered formation had been a fatal mistake. It caused the bombers to be strung out, sacrificing defensive fire power. Debriefings by all three groups revealed innumerable errors in both the planning and execution of the mission.

A mission to Hamburg on July 25 brought about sharp defensive action from the Luftwaffe and cost the 384th Bomb Group seven aircraft, nearly half of the fifteen that were lost by the 1st Bomb Wing. The 379th Bomb Group lost two B-17s, but had one come home through the concerted effort of crew members of a Fortress named *Judy Bea*.

The pilot of this aircraft was Lt. Willis Carlisle, a big, strapping 200-pounder. His copilot was a little wiry guy by the name of Lieutenant Bigler, whom he called "Big." Though they fought and swore at each other, Big refused to take a crew of his own and stayed on to fly with Carlisle.

As the B-17s approached the target, they came under attack from fighters. On one of the initial passes, Carlisle was hit and killed by a burst of 20mm fire. The fire that killed Carlisle knocked out the oxygen system on the right side of the flight deck. Carlisle slumped over and fell against Lieutenant Bigler. Realizing that he might pass out from lack of oxygen, Bigler trimmed the plane and

by holding the pilot off with one hand, he kept the bomber in formation with the other hand. After making the bomb run, Bigler called for help over the intercom.

When Lt. Joe Glazer, the bombardier, arrived, Technical Sergeant Tyler, the top turret gunner, was holding the pilot off the controls. Glazer switched the oxygen control for Bigler to emergency, but it was out. He then stripped off the pilot's mask and put it on Bigler. By this time Tyler was turning blue, so Bigler gave his walkaround bottle to him and sent him back up to the top turret to ward off fighter attacks.

Glazer was getting weak trying to hold Carlisle's body off the controls, so he had to get down on the catwalk to find an oxygen outlet that worked. Then one of the waist gunners came forward with four bottles and Glazer took them and returned to the flight deck. The pilot's body then slumped over and the aircraft went into a steep dive. Before Tyler and Glazer could remove the pilot's body from his seat, they had dropped to 8,500ft and oxygen was no longer necessary.

Glazer settled down in the pilot's seat, and he and Bigler brought the Fortress home.

For a similar act of courage, F/O John C. Morgan won the Medal of Honor on July 26, 1943. Morgan was flying as copilot with the 92nd Bomb Group on a B-17 named *Ruthie II* en route to bomb Hanover when the aircraft was attacked by Focke-Wulf 190s. When the fighters made their first pass, pilot Lt. Robert L. Campbell had his skull split open by enemy fire. Immediately after being hit Campbell slumped over the controls, grasping the yoke tightly. Morgan seized the controls and doggedly fought to keep the plane in formation while he tried to keep the pain-crazed pilot off the controls with the other hand. Desperately, Morgan called for help, but the intercom was shot out. When he received no response he assumed that the majority of the crew must have bailed out.

At the same time that the pilot was hit, the top turret gunner fell from his position down into the nose with his arm all but severed. The navigator realized that the man would quickly die without medical attention. The nose hatch was opened, and with great difficulty the navigator managed to push the gunner out with his parachute unfurled in his

A copilot's view of a feathered prop on the number four engine. Note the oil streaks back over the nacelle. USAAF

arms. Miraculously, the canopy opened and the gunner was later reported to be taken as a prisoner of war.

Meanwhile, Morgan continued to fight off the efforts of the pilot as he struggled to stay in formation. Rather than take a chance to run for home in the face of heavy enemy attacks, Morgan chose to fly on with the group. After two hours during which *Ruthie II* completed the mission with the rest of the B-17s, Morgan was finally discovered by navigator Lieutenant Koske, who helped remove the mortally wounded pilot from his seat and into the nose of the aircraft.

Weather and a new weapon by the Luftwaffe spelled disaster for a number of 8th Air Force Fortresses on July 28. The target was Oschersleben, but an appreciable number of the 4th Bomb Wing B-17s aborted the mission when layers of high clouds menaced the formations and several aircraft became separated from their units. Also spelling trouble for the bombers were the Fw 190s and Bf 110s that were equipped with rockets. These sizeable missiles were carried in tubes under the wings of the enemy aircraft and weighed about 250lb. They carried a 21lb warhead that had a preset range of about 1,200 yards, which was outside the range of the .50 caliber guns on the B-17s. One of the missiles hit a 385th Bomb Group Fortress which in turn crashed into two other B-17s in its formation; all three aircraft went down to their destruction.

Other Fortress formations were broken up in their attempt to avoid the missiles and wend their way through the clouds. The 96th Bomb Group came under very heavy attack during this period and lost a number of its aircraft, including its lead ship, before it reached the German coast. Most of the crew members who were forced to bail out or ditch in the sea were lost.

Some of the 96th Fortresses formed on the rear of the 94th Bomb Group which fought its way on in to the target, the Focke-Wulf assembly plant, at Oschersleben. As one of the 96th crew members recalled going in from the initial point of the bomb run, "Fighters were pressing home savage attacks. A Fort broke out in flames, across all four engines. I saw five chutes open. A German fighter exploded—a ball of orange flame hanging in the air. Another Fort twisted out of control, an engine burning, its tail sheared off . . . "

The 96th Bomb Group returned to base at Snetterton to find seven of its aircraft missing. The 4th Bomb Wing lost fifteen of its Fortresses on the mission.

August 17, 1943, is a date that will live forever in the annals of aerial warfare. It was on that date that 8th Air Force flew its historic dual mission to Regensburg and Schweinfurt. Regensburg was the home of the Messerschmitt factory, manufacturers of the vaunted Bf 109, and Schweinfurt was the location of three ball-bearing factories, the essential components of everything mechanical in the Third Reich. To eliminate these centers would cut deeply into German aircraft and armament production. If the two plants could be completely destroyed, it could shorten the war in Europe.

The missions had been in the planning stage for some time, and the planners knew that strikes so deep into Germany without fighter escort would bring with it heavy casualties in the bomber force. In order to minimize losses, yet enable the missions to be flown, a plan was formulated that would send the 1st and the 4th Bomb Wings against the targets simultaneously. The plan called for the Regensburg force—which would be provided with P-47 Thunderbolt escort—to cross the coast of Holland at approximately 0830 hours. The Schweinfurt force would be 15 minutes behind them. It was contemplated that the Regensburg force would draw the majority of fighter opposition, thus reducing the hazards for the Schweinfurt force. To further confuse the Luftwaffe, the Regensburg force would turn south and continue on to bases in North Africa. This should string out the Luftwaffe, and make attacks against the Schweinfurt force minimal as they did their bombing and returned to England.

Unfortunately, the operation did not go as planned. On the morning of August 17, weather did not cooperate. The staff of VIII Bomber Command debated canceling or postponing the operation, but finally made a decision that would prove lethal to the crews aboard the B-17s. The Regensburg force would take off as scheduled, while the Schweinfurt force would not get airborne until over three and a half hours later!

Col. Curtis LeMay led the Regensburg force, flying in the lead aircraft of the 96th Bomb Group. Its B-17s began to get off the ground at 0621 hours. The bombers formed up and headed out across the English Channel. They were provided with escort by the 353rd and 56th Fighter Group P-47s. There was some interception by the Luftwaffe, but no great damage was done until the Thunderbolts ran low on fuel and were forced to break off the escort and return to England.

Once the P-47s left, the Luftwaffe began their attacks in earnest. They not only used the head-on attack, but also came in from every angle. Some came straight down on the combat boxes, diving all the way from the high squadron to the low. Twin-engine Messerschmitt Bf 110s and Junkers Ju 88s sat out of .50 caliber range and fired rockets into the formation. The historian of the 100th Bomb Group reported the air battle as follows:

"It happened ten miles southwest of Antwerp. The Germans came in fast. The Fortresses turrets ground in azimuth and elevation, and short bursts stitched through the sky. From the initial moment of near-terror until the assault ceased two hours later, more than two hundred attacks were pressed against the Hundredth. There was desperation in the air as the Luftwaffe piled in and slugged it out. They seemed to anticipate the route, and later, many men confessed that they felt sharp fear of the formation being caught and trapped. As the aircraft crossed into the Reich proper the attacks seemed to increase in intensity. The group rocked under the constant pressure of individual fighter attacks from every clock position. It would scarcely have helped had the men known that the struggle was still not anywhere near its peak. Forts and fighters lit the sky with a series of brilliant explosions and the debris-cluttered air seemed to hold nothing but death and the realization that death was inevitable.

"A couple of Jerry twin-engine jobs stood off to the side as though sitting in on a wake and sent word to their friends further up the road to prepare a hot welcome for the invaders as they drove deeper into the land.

"The B-17s shook with the fury of their .50s as the gunners became inured to destruction. Ammunition ran low in many ships and belts were transported from one position to another. Outside the windows, parachutes descended in swaying patterns and slow motion, an odd contrast to the swift and jagged geometric patterns of aircraft parts that plummeted down. It was impossible to keep track of any near order of events. The entire flight became a kaleidoscopic dream of nightmarish quality, a scene in ugly colors of smoke, fire and the yellow, red and black nosed enemy etched against the incongruously peaceful blue backdrop of the sky."

Of the twenty-four Fortresses that were lost on the mission to Regensburg, nine of them that fell were from the 100th Bomb Group. Also hard hit on the mission was the 390th Bomb Group, which lost six aircraft.

It was, no doubt, fortunate that the Regensburg force turned south, for the Luftwaffe would have been ready to intercept them once more on the way home. The B-17s journeyed down to North Africa where they landed, but much to their chagrin they found that

there was little there to welcome them or assist them with their damaged aircraft.

The Schweinfurt force did not become airborne until after 1100 hours. They, too, had two groups of Thunderbolts escorting them in, but when the escort departed, the Luftwaffe, which had already done extensive damage that day, was fully alert and waiting for them.

The Luftwaffe appeared just before the Fortresses reached Eupen where they were to have rendezvoused with the Thunderbolts of the 4th Fighter Group. The P-47s did not appear, and Focke-Wulf 190s of I/JG 26 attacked the low squadron of the 91st Bomb Group.

Lt. Don Von Der Heyde's B-17 was hit and went down spinning. Only two men would survive.

The real battle began when the Luftwaffe attacked the 381st Bomb Group. S/Sgt. Kenneth Stone, a ball turret gunner in the lead ship, reported the following: " . . . Our fighter escort left us near the German border, and we entered southern Germany protected now only by our own guns. Ten minutes after our fighter escort had turned back, enemy formations appeared from out of the clouds. There were over a hundred: Messerschmitt 109s, Focke-Wulf 190s, and Messerschmitt 110s. I watched them circle our group, sizing us up. They separated and formed in flights of fifteen abreast about 5,000 yards in front of our plane.

"The first flight came in head-on with their 20mm guns blazing. I fired at the plane nearest my position and gave

Sunrise for a maintenance crew. These men knew no limits to which they would not go to get their Fortress airborne. 306th BG Assn.

him a short burst. Four more flights came in head-on and scattered through our formation. Lieutenant Painter and Captain Nelson, who were flying behind us as deputy leader, fell out of formation and left the group with one engine blazing. The crew bailed out. Three more planes dropped out of formation, and parachutes billowed from them. Fighters were going down right and left. The Fortress gunners were deadly accurate. The plane of my former copilot, Lieutenant Darrow, had one engine knocked out, but managed to keep up with the remaining formation.

57

"The enemy fighters finally departed for their bases to refuel and prepare to meet us on our way back to England. Our group had already lost four planes. As we approached the target we were met by flak. The German gunners put up a barrage over the target, and we had to fly straight through the flak. This proved to be disastrous to some planes. Our bombardier, Lieutenant Hester, opened the bomb bay doors and dropped our deadly cargo. I watched the bombs plummet down and hit the target. The ball-bearing plants were well plastered with bomb hits, and smoke rose high and fast.

"Our only thought now was to get back safely to our base. About fifteen minutes after leaving the target, enemy fighters were sighted coming in towards our right. They again attacked head-on, five abreast. This method of attack was new to us and was very effective. Campbell, our radio operator, asked permission to leave his radio to fire his gun; it was okay with Captain Briggs. Our right wing man, Lieutenant Jarvis, had his number three engine hit by enemy guns and it caught fire. The waist gunner waved to us as they dropped out of formation. Chutes were all over the sky—white ones and the brown chutes of enemy fighter pilots.

"Sweat was running down my face even though the temperature was thirty degrees below zero. I was afraid that we would never see England again; the odds were too much against us. I saw more fighters—miles to the right—and heading our way. I began praying to God and asking him for courage to see this through. The fighters came closer and closer and began attacking the pride of the Luftwaffe. Our escort had finally arrived . . . Hallelujah!"

Also being shot to pieces in the lead formation was the 91st Bomb Group. They managed to hold themselves together for the first 15 minutes of the attacks; after that, they were downed one by one. Amazingly, the lead aircraft flown by Lt. Col. Clemens Wurzbach, the group commander, survived.

Thirty-six B-17s from the 1st Bomb Wing were lost that day, including

96th Bomb Group Fortresses taxi out for take-off turns en route to another mission over Europe. Ethell

59

eleven from the 381st Bomb Group and ten from the 91st Bomb Group. This, coupled with the Regensburg losses, brought a total of sixty Fortresses lost in the attacks. Although gunners on the bombers claimed 288 enemy fighters destroyed, they actually downed twenty-one. Escorting P-47s are credited with fourteen enemy fighters, and RAF Spitfires got another seven.

It was thought from the strike photos that the Messerschmitt factory at Regensburg was completely destroyed. After digging through the wreckage, however, the Germans found that most of the machine tools were undamaged, and the factory was reconstructed. The Germans officially estimated that some 800 to 1,000 fighters were lost as a result of the raid, which was equivalent to six to eight weeks' production. Damage at Schweinfurt was even less, but it did prompt the manufacturers to begin doling out ball-bearing production to small manufacturers scattered across Germany. This made it impossible for the Allies to put a complete halt to production.

In the massive air battles that took place in 1943 it is usually related, particularly in unit histories and such, that the fighters encountered were either the "Abbeville Kids," "Goering's select group of aces," or "Goering's yellow-nose elite." While the Luftwaffe fighter units were very good, none of these descriptions is accurate. The group usually referred to as the Abbeville Kids consisted of the fighters of JG 26, which was based on the French coast in the Abbeville area. While the pilots in this unit in 1943 were largely veteran combat aviators, they were not all high-scoring aces nor were they picked by Goering for this unit or for any other fighter wing for that matter. The German fighters that were encountered during 1943 were largely from JG 1, JG 2, JG 3, JG 11, and JG 26. A Jagdgeschwader could be composed of up to twelve squadrons, and the squadrons were usually three to a group. However, not all JGs in action in the West were composed of all three groups at this time. During the summer of 1943, the Luftwaffe pulled in ZGs (wings of twin-engine Bf 110 destroyers) to aid in the defense of the Reich. When necessary, twin-engine night fighters from the NJGs (night-fighter wings) were pressed into service.

The Eighth Air Force did not attempt another strike deep into Germany until September 6, 1943, when it set out on a maximum effort to strike the SKF instrument bearing plant at Stuttgart. Gen. H. H. Arnold was in England on an inspection trip and, undoubtedly, General Eaker wanted to show him that the Eighth Air Force still could successfully penetrate and bomb a target deep in the Third Reich.

The 96th Bomb Group set out leading its wing and once France was crossed without fighter opposition, it was felt that it would be a particularly good mission. When they reached the German border, however, a front of clouds appeared. The Germans surrounded the target area with smoke pots, further obscuring the target. On the first bomb run, the target was not visible, so the bombers swung around through the flak for a second bomb run. Then the Luftwaffe decided to put in its appearance.

The 388th Bomb Group was picked by the German fighter pilots to receive their undivided attention. More than one hundred fighters attacked the group, which desperately repelled attack after attack for an extended period of time. The first heavy attack consisted of fighters forming up two or three miles in front of the bombers and then coming in level from eleven o'clock to one o'clock. For the first 5 minutes, the attacking fighters assumed a traffic pattern attacking mostly from the left at eleven o'clock. They trailed each other in, slightly stepped up, at about twenty-second intervals. At 300 to 400 yards the fighters would start their roll and make their pass at the lead squadron. After the low squadron of bombers was eliminated, the traffic pattern was shifted over to the right. Some attacks were pressed as close as fifty to seventy-five yards.

The 388th Group lost eleven of its Fortresses on the mission and suffered one crew member killed and two seriously wounded on the aircraft that returned.

The lead squadron of the 303rd Bomb Group led the 41st Combat Wing, with Brig. Gen. Robert F. Travis, new wing commander, in the lead aircraft. When the wing arrived and found the target covered by clouds and smoke, it began to orbit. Many of the Fortresses were low on fuel by this time, so it was imperative that they drop their bombs

and head for England. Even so, Travis kept leading the formation through steep banks to one side and then the other, making it impossible for some of the aircraft to maintain formation. Some were forced to salvo their bombs to keep up. When bombs were finally dropped, it was a known fact that many of the B-17s did not have enough fuel left to return to England.

Twelve B-17s were forced to ditch in the English Channel with 118 crew members being picked up by air-sea rescue. Two other Fortresses crash-landed in England. Four badly damaged bombers made it to Switzerland, and one crashed in a Swiss lake. All in all, the mission had been an expensive fiasco.

September 1943 saw the arrival of the first B-17Gs in the Eighth Air Force. The engines were a newer and more powerful modification, and there were numerous minor changes made in the aircraft that improved its overall performance. The two most important new features on the G model were the chin turret, which originally had been introduced on the YB-40, and staggered waist windows that were covered with plexiglass. These additions and modifications gave the nose of the aircraft the firepower that it had needed for so long, and the improved waist windows cut the chilling winds aloft in the rear of the aircraft that had resulted in so many severe cases of frostbite. Additionally, the oxygen hoses and communication leads for the waist gunners were placed on their respective sides of the fuselage and no longer did the gunners have tangled lines coming down from the ceiling of the fuselage, nor were they bumping rears constantly, which tended to frustrate action on either side.

Several other innovations were introduced to the 8th Air Force during this period. For some weeks, several Fortresses had been assigned to the new 813th Bomb Squadron. This unit was formed to indoctrinate crews using British H2S radars that allowed accurate blind bombing when the target was obscured by clouds or smoke. Initially, the radar sets were installed under the Fortresses' nose, but the radar was installed in place of the ball turret, in a retractable housing, in later aircraft. This set, called "Mickey" by the Eighth Air Force crew members, was used in radar bombing of targets from the fall of 1943

on. The crews from the 813th Bomb Squadron, called "Pathfinders" or "PFF," went from one unit to another performing their duties.

Other innovations that came to light during the fall of 1943 were "window" and "carpet." Window consisted of strips of tinfoil about 1/16in wide and 11in long. These strips were dropped from the Fortresses beginning at the initial point of the bomb run. They tended to appear as thousands of targets on the

Royal Flush *from the 401st Bomb Squadron, 91st Bomb Group takes off from Bassingborn on November 3, 1943, en route to Wilhelmshaven.* USAAF

German radar screens, and often confused the radars that aimed the flak batteries.

Carpet was an airborne transmitter that could be used to jam ground radar frequencies. This was another attempt to reduce the effectiveness of the flak batteries which were beginning to take a higher toll of the bombers.

The Pathfinder crews of the 813th Bomb Squadron took on their first task on September 27, 1943. Two B-17s were assigned to the 1st Air Division and two to the 3rd Air Division's to accompany the bombers on a mission to Emden. The mission was not really successful, though, as one of the Pathfinders assigned to the 1st had his radar go out and the 1st Air Division second aircraft had its radar set hit by flak on the way to the target. One of the 3rd Air Division operators found his radar faulty, so the crew did not go on the mission. The other aircraft made the mission and marked the target, which was cloud covered. The target was bombed, but later reconnaissance photos showed that most of the bombs had hit wide of the mark.

October 8 found the Fortresses on their way to Bremen. The 3rd Air Division went in over the North Sea, followed by the B-24s, which veered off to bomb Vegesack. The 1st Air Division attacked Bremen after overflying Holland. Clouds caused several formations to bomb targets of opportunity. Those that did fly over Bremen encountered some of the heaviest flak of the war. The 100th Bomb Group, after encountering fighter attacks before the bomb run, was hard hit by flak and lost several of their aircraft to the barrage. All total, seven of the 100th's B-17s failed to return from the mission.

All of the units participating came under very heavy attack from Luftwaffe fighters. The 381st Bomb Group was particularly hard hit, losing seven of their B-17s to Focke-Wulf 190s before they reached the target. One of the 381st's aircraft that did get home that day was *Tinker Toy*. This Fortress had come under heavy attack by enemy fighters. On the first run, the fighters put 20mm shells in the pilot's side of the

Mechanics hard at work getting the engines of Boss Lady *ready for another mission.* Ethell

cockpit and decapitated Lt. William J. Minerich. Copilot Lt. Thomas Sellers took over the controls.

At the same time, the nose had been blown off the aircraft and the bombardier and navigator fought fighter attacks in the freezing blast. A second fighter pass hit Lieutenant Sellers in the arm and left him flying with one arm. The navigator came up and assisted Sellers in bringing the aircraft home.

October 9 saw VIII Bomber Command perform one of the most successful diversionary missions in its history. All three air divisions started out across the North Sea, and the German controllers were at a loss to determine their destination. It seems they decided that all were destined for Anklam, the home of the Arado aircraft factory. This proved to be the destination of the 1st Air Division, but the majority of the 3rd Air Division went on to strike the Focke-Wulf factory at Marienburg while other 3rd Division B-17s went to Gdynia and the B-24s of the 2nd Air Division went to Danzig.

The missions were carried out at medium altitudes of 11,000 to 16,000ft, for it was known that there was no heavy flak concentration at Marienburg. The 3rd Division did an excellent job of bombing there, and damage to the Focke-Wulf plant was extensive. The Fortresses of the 1st Air Division also did a good job at Anklam, but they certainly accomplished their job of getting the fighters off the Marienburg bombers, for they ran into the fight of their lives.

A number of single-engine fighters were encountered after the B-17s crossed the Danish coast and some losses were suffered. It was after the bombs had been dropped and the formations were on their way home that the massive attacks took place. First, there were twin-engine Bf 110s, Bf 210s, Ju 88s, and even Dornier Do 217s standing off to fire their rockets in the bomber formations. The 91st and the 351st Groups took the brunt of the attacks, each losing five aircraft on the mission. Some formations were under attack for as much as three and a half hours. The crews of the 91st Bomb Group considered the attacks "their Schweinfurt."

October 10 marked the first time that the bombers of the 8th Air Force had ever been given a civilian target. The aiming point was the center of Munster,

Germany. The city was a railroad hub and it was thought that by striking at the city, many rail workers would become their targets and the rail system in the Ruhr valley would suffer accordingly.

Sixteen groups of B-17s took off en route to the target with the 13th Combat Wing of the 3rd Air Division consisting of the 95th, 100th, and 390th Bomb Groups leading. P-47s escorted the bombers up to the point that they were 9 minutes from Munster. Due to ground fog on their base, the relieving Thunderbolts were not able to make their rendezvous. This spelled disaster for the lead wing.

As the Fortresses pushed on, they faced the greatest concentration of Luftwaffe fighters they had ever encountered. On their first pass they concentrated on the 100th Group which was flying low group in the wing. On the first pass, eight to ten enemy fighters went directly through the Fortress formation from twelve o'clock level. The first attack took three B-17s out of the 100th Group formation. From then on, the enemy continued to barrel through the lead groups in waves while their twin-engine fighters stood off to the side and rear and lobbed their rockets into the bombers.

As they came off the target the 100th Group Fortress, *Sexy Suzy, Mother of Ten,* piloted by Lt. William Beddow, collided with a Bf 109. The crew members only knew that something had hit the left wing and everything was on fire. Four of the crew members managed to bail out of the inferno. Lieutenant Beddow did not survive.

This collision spiraled into a second Fortress, *Sweater Girl,* which went down as a result of the crash. Its six survivors bailed out to become prisoners of war.

Of the 100th Group's aircraft that came off the target, a few of the remaining aircraft dove for the deck in a vain attempt to escape the fighter attacks and run for home. None of them made it. The only survivor of the thirteen 100th Group B-17s was *Royal Flush* being flown by Lt. Robert "Rosie" Rosenthal. Although one engine had been knocked out, his aircraft bombed the target and then became the target of numerous fighter attacks. The number three engine was hit and had to be feathered, and the oxygen system was almost completely destroyed. Lieutenant Rosenthal

managed to bring the aircraft back home on two engines and put it down in a gathering fog.

While the 100th Group had lost twelve aircraft, the 390th had lost eight and the 95th Group of the 13th Wing lost five. The Luftwaffe decided to knock out the lead wing and they just about did it. The bombing destroyed large sections of the city and knocked out its electrical system completely. The intensity of the air battle is indicated by the high claims made by the crew members of the Fortresses. The B-17 crews claimed 183 enemy aircraft destroyed on the mission. German records show that only twenty-four of their fighters went down that day.

October 14 would become another fateful day in "Black Week" for the Eighth Air Force. The mission was the second attempt to knock out the ball-bearing factories at Schweinfurt. The official publication *The Combined Bomber Offensive* stated: "All told more than 300 enemy aircraft participated in the battle and these made 700 separate attacks on the bombers during the principal fight.

"The first enemy maneuver was to attack from the front at very close range with a screen of single-engine fighters firing 20mm cannon, and machine guns. Following this screen were a number of twin-engine fighters in formation, firing rockets from projectors suspended under the wings. The rocket-firing craft began their attacks at a distance and did not come in nearly so close as the single-engine fighters. The Fortress formations were subjected to great numbers of rocket projectiles.

"After the single-engine fighters had made their initial assault, they refueled and returned to the battle, this time attacking from all directions in an attempt to confuse the gunners in the heavy bombers. Then followed the second effort of the enemy twin-engine fighters, which attacked principally from the front and rear.

"The rocket-firing craft seemed to concentrate upon a single combat wing until their ammunition was exhausted. After these maneuvers, all enemy fighters centered their attention on the bombers that had been crippled by the organized attacks . . . "

The 305th Bomb Group was the hardest hit that day en route to Schweinfurt, losing a quarter of the total lost

by the Eighth Air Force, fifteen out of eighteen planes. "I watched from my left window as the 305th, flying low and to our left, away from the other groups, lost one plane after another," related Capt. Charles Schoolfield, leader of the 306th Bomb Group formation. "First they got the last plane and then chewed up through the formation until they almost completely destroyed it."

In the fury of the assault it was difficult for Schoolfield, as the group leader, or Lt. Curtis L. Dunlap, flying as tail gunner and formation observer, to keep track of what was happening. When the shooting slackened, Schoolfield was shocked to learn that he had only five planes left. The 306th birds huddled together for mutual protection as they came down the forty-second bomb run, tailed only by the 92nd Bomb Group. The 306th dropped its 1,000lb bombs, and sixteen of them landed within a 1,920ft circle.

Having bombed on a heading of forty-five degrees, the planes came around to the left and headed west on a withdrawal route that took them south of Paris and then north toward England. Schoolfield's badly damaged plane staggered along as the leader. At one point, with a fire in the number three engine, Schoolfield had actually pushed the alarm bell switch, but nothing happened, so he gave up thoughts of bailing out and tried to keep the plane flying.

Later, Maj. Gen. Orval Anderson, in conversation with Schoolfield, said that the withdrawal route had been his idea; both agreed that had the withdrawal been along the line of penetration, the casualties would have been much more than the sixty lost by the Eighth Air Force. This represented 20 percent of

Knockout Dropper is another illustration of the varied art on Eighth Air Force noses. Ethell

the planes taking off in the raid. In the annals of warfare, and particularly to those who met an unwanted fate on October 14, the day will be known forever as "Black Thursday." Indeed, it was for the ten 306th crews who gave their all on the mission.

Of the one hundred men who did not return to Thurleigh that afternoon, thirty-five died on the mission or later of wounds. Sixty-five went to prison camp.

The 305th Bomb Group led by Maj. Charles G. Y. Normand had its troubles as was observed by Captain Schoolfield. Over Frankfurt, twin-engine Bf 210 fighters appeared astern and again lobbed rockets. By now, the 364th Bomb

Squadron had lost all seven of its airplanes. Still, the enemy attack picked up in intensity. Soon all four 366th Bomb Squadron planes, flying the high squadron, fell to the flak and the fighters.

Major Normand watched in horror as plane after plane was shot down. The sky was filled with burning aircraft and the parachutes of the men that had escaped from them. As the remnants of the group turned on the initial point for the bombing, Normand's bombardier called for a separate bomb run. He didn't know that only three planes were left in the formation and one of them was on fire.

Lt. Raymond Bullock flew the aircraft that was on fire, a Fortress named *Sundown Sal*. The B-17 had been hit in the left wing by a 20mm shell, which started the blaze. Bullock held the B-17 in formation until the bombs were dropped. Immediately after the bomb run, he left the formation and told his crew to bail out. All became prisoners.

In the final tally for the 305th Bomb Group, the 364th Squadron lost all seven of its aircraft; the 365th Squadron lost two; and the 366th Squadron lost four. Two 365th planes returned. Of the 130 crew members lost, thirty-six had been killed. The 87 percent loss for the day left the group devastated.

The assessment of damage at the target was originally stated to be total destruction. Unfortunately, this was not true. While considerable damage had been done, in no way did it put the Germans out of the ball-bearing business. However, the damage forced the Germans to speed up the dispersion of the industry to the countryside.

The loss of sixty bombers on the mission further swelled the loss figure for October. In all, the Eighth Air Force lost 176 B-17s during this month. Bomber crew morale hit a new low. Never did they think that they would be asked to fight their way to the target and back under such overwhelming opposition. Of course, it was hurting the Luftwaffe as well, but many of their pilots were recovered and back in the air the following day. The one thing that the American Fortress crews had proven beyond a doubt was that they had the guts to

A colorful formation of B-17s over England. Defensive positions can be clearly seen. Ethell

press on to their targets regardless of the odds. They were never turned back by the enemy!

There was little comfort for the bomber crews in the message that Chief of Staff Gen. H. H. Arnold released to the press following the Schweinfurt mission. The message read: "Regardless of our losses, I'm ready to send replacements of planes and crews and continue building up our strength. The opposition isn't nearly what it was, and we are wearing them down. The loss of 60 American bombers in the Schweinfurt raid was incidental."

If the opposition wasn't nearly what it was, the crews of the Fortresses felt they must have been hallucinating!

To further compound the odds that the bomber crews had to face, by November 1943 the Luftwaffe had reinforced its fighter aircraft strength in the west to 800. The good news was that drop tanks for the Thunderbolts were finally beginning to become more available, and two groups of P-38 Lightnings arrived. The P-38 would never become the victor that it was in other theaters because its performance suffered in the extreme cold of northwestern Europe, but it could provide deep escort. The best news was that the P-51 Mustang would arrive in England in December. This aircraft, with its superb performance, could also go all the way with the bombers regardless of the target. The days of Luftwaffe superiority were definitely numbered.

The Eighth Air Force made some forays into Germany in November and completed a long mission to Norway during the month, but enemy opposition was negligible. Most of the missions over Germany encountered bad weather and used PFF bombing if the bombs were dropped.

December also got off to a slow start, but it did find the P-38s aloft. On December 5, the P-51s got in the picture when the 354th Fighter Group escorted the bombers to targets in France. The next sharp action with the Luftwaffe came on December 16 when the bombers went to Bremen. The 96th Bomb Group put up thirty-six B-17s in an A Group and a B Group, but all was not fated to go well for the men from Snetterton that day.

The A Group fared the better of the two groups, but lost two B-17s to a mid-air collision. It happened over the North Sea, and there were only two survivors.

The B Group was hit by fifteen Focke-Wulf 190s that came roaring out of the sun. The first two B-17s went down following an attack on an aircraft that had an engine shot completely loose from its wing. The engine fell down on the aircraft below, and before it was all over the two Fortresses became tangled and fell together.

As the bombers became scattered the fighters jumped on them individually, and three more were downed, making a total of five B-17s downed by the Luftwaffe. As the bombers came home they lost another Fortress, one of the most historic aircraft in the group.

Fertile Myrtle III had led the Regensburg mission with Colonel LeMay at the controls, and had led the 3rd Air Division to Schweinfurt on October 14. It came back over England from the Bremen mission badly shot up, with all control surfaces damaged and a number of control cables severed. The fin was slashed and there were a number of large holes in the fuselage and wings. The pilot, Capt. Tom Kenny, gave the order and the crew bailed out. *Myrtle* crashed near Norwick.

The bombers went back to Bremen on December 20, and it was on this mission that a second enlisted crew member on a B-17 won the Medal of Honor. The 303rd Bomb Group entered heavy flak over the target, and *Jersey Bounce Jr.* was hit and left the formation. Number one engine was on fire, but the pilot, Lt. John Henderson, and instructor pilot Capt. Merle Hunderford, who was flying copilot, managed to roll the aircraft into the wing and blow out the fire.

Then the fighters began to attack. One came in from six o'clock and got in a telling burst that seriously wounded the tail gunner, Sgt. George Buske, and also

put shrapnel in the legs of Sgt. Forrest Vosler, the radio operator. Vosler says that he went over to his chair and sat down, but decided that was not the thing to do and got back up and manned his machine gun.

Fighters continued to fly their attacks with the gunners fighting them off and apparently scoring good hits and perhaps downing some of them. Vosler had a twin-engine fighter come in from the rear so close he could see the pilot's face. A good burst from his guns and the German pilot dove down and went beneath the Fortress.

Then a 20mm shell went into the radio room, followed down the side of Vosler's gun, and exploded, showering Vosler with shrapnel. He was particularly hard hit in the eyes and face. Blinded in one eye and bloody all over, he felt that his time had come but Vosler went over to his radio table and apparently went into a state of shock for a time.

By this time, the pilots had the B-17 down on the deck, and the able crew members were throwing out everything they could to lighten the load. The wounded tail gunner had been brought forward to the radio room and Vosler sat at his radio, blinded, but able to carry out emergency procedures on his set. As soon as the Fortress was over water, Vosler began sending out SOS signals. They were acknowledged, and air-sea rescue services were put in motion.

The aircraft was ditched not far off the coast of England and all the men except the pilots went out the radio hatch. The tail gunner, still unconscious, was put out on the wing. While boarding the dinghies the tail gunner almost slipped into the sea, but the nearly blind Vosler grabbed the unconscious gunner and held on until he could be placed in the raft. Only then did Vosler get in the dinghy.

The entire crew was picked up by a ship shortly thereafter and taken back to England. Vosler and the tail gunner were sent to the hospital. Vosler was later returned to the United States for treatment. He remained blind for a time, but once the damaged right eye was removed, he began to regain sight in his other eye. For his fortitude and devotion to his job and assistance to his crew, though critically wounded, Vosler was awarded the Medal of Honor.

As 1943 came to a close, the Eighth Air Force could look back on its accomplishments with great pride. It had proved that daylight bombing could be successful. Although the Luftwaffe had taken its toll and October 1943 had proven to be such a bad month, the crews on the bombers continued to fight their way through. If their claims for enemy fighters destroyed had been true, there would have been no Luftwaffe left to oppose them. Yet, they had cost the enemy hundreds of their best trained pilots and aircraft. They had forced the Luftwaffe to move a number of its fighter units from the Eastern Front where they were desperately needed, and from the Mediterranean where Germany had lost North Africa and Sicily, and had seen Italy invaded. At the beginning of 1943, only four B-17 units were in operation. By the end of 1943 there were eighteen Fortress units operating, plus the B-24s of the 2nd Air Division. Instead of 100 heavy bombers ready to launch an offensive in January 1943, the Eighth Air Force could put over 600 aircraft aloft in January 1944.

The Eighth Air Force would soon grow to the extent that it could send more than 1,000 bombers and another 1,000 fighters to escort them to any target in Germany. The daylight bombing offensive was ready to dominate the skies over northwestern Europe.

Chapter 6

Big Week, Big B, and Beyond

January 6, 1944, brought a momentous announcement to VIII Bomber Command. Lt. Gen. Ira Eaker, who had commanded the Eighth Air Force since its inception, was to be relieved of his command and would be replaced by Lt. Gen. James H. Doolittle, who had been air commander in the Mediterranean. Gen. Carl "Tooey" Spaatz was named commander of strategic bombing in Europe and would command not only Doolittle, but also General Eaker who would take over as commander of the air forces in the Mediterranean. VIII Bomber Command would cease to exist, and bombing activities would be commanded directly by General Doolittle.

For some time, the bombers of the Eighth Air Force had been trying to launch a deep penetration into Germany and it was deemed that January 11 would be a good day. The 1st Air Division was slated to strike the Focke-Wulf plant at Oschersleben and aircraft facilities at Halberstadt. The 3rd Air Division was to strike at Brunswick and Osnabruck.

Leading the 1st Division was the 303rd Bomb Group, and division commander Brig. Gen. Robert Travis was in the lead aircraft. The formations were assembled and were out over the Channel and over the enemy coast on schedule. General Travis reported: "The fighters started their attacks at the Zuider Zee despite our fighter escort and came

at us in bunches. Our first attacks were four Fw 190s, the next was thirty Fw 190s, the next was twelve, and they just kept coming. They attacked straight through the formation from all angles without even rolling over. They came in from all sides and it was quite apparent that they were out to stop the formation from ever reaching the target."

As usual, the single-engine fighters came in from head-on and came to within seventy-five yards of the Fortresses before they broke away. As the fight became more heated, collisions also occurred that resulted from the Luftwaffe pilot pressing his attack too close, or perhaps he had been killed or wounded in his attack and his aircraft just kept coming until it smashed into one of the B-17s.

Somewhere in the vicinity of Dummer Lake, General Travis reported that the weather was deteriorating rapidly over England, so the mission was being recalled. The 2nd and 3rd Divisions turned back, but the 1st Division was so close to the target that Travis ordered them to continue the mission. Unfortunately, the escorting fighters received the recall and many of them turned and headed for home while the 1st Division Fortresses continued eastward.

The enemy fighters continued to come at the lead formation. Amazingly, General Travis' aircraft *The Eight Ball* did not go down, although the aircraft

surrounding it did. The Focke-Wulfs got the Mickey radar aircraft on the first pass and then took out the leader of the second element and his wingman from the lead squadron. Leading the 1st Division, the 303rd Bomb Group's bombs struck the target well and apparently did extensive damage, but the intense air battle cost them eleven aircraft lost and most of those that did return suffered damage.

The rest of the Fortresses of the 1st Combat Wing also took heavy losses, with the 381st Bomb Group losing eight aircraft and the 91st Bomb Group losing five. One of the 381st B-17s was lost in a collision with an enemy fighter.

Although many of the escorting fighters turned back when the recall was sounded, others remained in the combat area. The outstanding event of the day was the performance of Maj. James H. Howard flying one of the new P-51 Mustangs of the 354th Fighter Group. He found the 401st Bomb Group under heavy attack and entered the fight alone. For over half an hour he battled all types of enemy aircraft and no doubt saved the Fortresses from a number of losses. The crew in the B-17s would confirm six enemy aircraft destroyed for him, but Howard would only accept credit for three. For his feat he was awarded the Medal of Honor.

The 3rd Division, which was headed for Brunswick, received its recall but in

70

Col. George L. Robinson with Princess Elizabeth at the christening of Rose of York. *306th BG Assn.*

view of the fact that the lead groups were only twenty-five miles from the target when it was received, flight leader Maj. Louis G. Thorup of the 94th Bomb Group decided to proceed. The 94th was initially unable to identify their target so they did a 360 degree circle and then went in and bombed. As they came off the target, eighteen Messerschmitt Bf 110s set up out of range and began firing rockets into the formation. Hits were scored on several Fortresses, and these damaged bombers were forced to leave the formation; then they were attacked by Focke-Wulf 190s.

Both the 94th Bomb Group and the 447th Bomb Group that accompanied them were under heavy attack for over an hour. The 94th lost eight of its B-17s while the 447th lost three.

The Eighth Air Force lost sixty B-17s for the day, and many of those returning would never fly again. The intensity of the air battle that day is indicated by the fact that the bomber crew members claimed 210 enemy aircraft destroyed. Actual Luftwaffe losses for the day were only thirty-nine, with thirty-one claims being made by the fighter escort.

The 94th Bomb Group took off on February 10, 1944, en route to Brunswick, and once more the Luftwaffe was waiting. The B-17s were attacked an hour from the target by a force of at least 150 Luftwaffe fighters, and as usual the attackers performed effectively with their head-on passes by single-engine fighters and rockets from the twin-engines. The B-17s were under attack for about two hours—from the Zuider Zee on the way in, to the Zuider Zee on the way out.

One veteran crew that didn't make it home that day was that of Lt. Don Anderson in *Good Time Cholley III*. Just before the initial point they were hit by 20mm shells between number three and

71

A beautiful profile photo of a B-17G at sunset over England. 306th BG Assn.

four engines. Fire broke out and the Fortress was forced to leave formation. Both waist gunners and the ball turret gunner were wounded. Anderson hit the bail-out bell and the navigator, bombardier, and top turret gunner bailed out. Meanwhile, two of the gunners were

looking after Sgt. Rex Smith who had been badly wounded. Anderson dropped down to 500ft and got the fire to die down, and decided to make a run for home.

However, Lady Luck was not with them. A stray Bf 109 appeared on the scene and although the wounded gunners did their utmost, the Fort was sprayed with fire from one end to the other. Anderson immediately told the crew they would have to bail out, but

then discovered that Smith was not able to do so.

Anderson and his copilot, Lt. Al Capie, began looking for a landing site. Just as they lined up on a field, another stray fighter came along looking for the cripple and once more the wounded gunners were engaged. This time, Sgt. Carl Evans was wounded and Sergeant Kremper was hit for the second time. The enemy fighter left the scene smoking, just before Anderson set down the

Fortress. All aboard were taken prisoner shortly after landing.

Once more, the Luftwaffe had taken a heavy toll of the B-17s of the 3rd Division. Twenty-nine out of 169 bombers dispatched had been lost for a 17 percent loss. Although 466 fighters had been launched, most of them missed their rendezvous which contributed heavily to the loss of the bombers.

For some weeks Gen. Carl Spaatz, commander of US Strategic Air Forces in Europe, had been planning a joint offensive in conjunction with the RAF against the German aircraft industry. The Eighth Air Force from England and the Fifteenth Air Force from Italy would strike the enemy installations during the day while the RAF would bomb them at night.

After weeks of waiting, the weather finally cleared sufficiently for what was to become known as "Big Week" to begin on February 20. The Eighth Air Force sent out over 400 B-17s from the 1st Bomb Division and 300 from the 3rd Bomb Division against aircraft factories and component plants in Germany. The 2nd Bomb Division of B-24s was also dispatched against similar targets. The Fifteenth Air Force was to have bombed

Regensburg at the same time, but icing conditions over the Alps prevented their mission.

Although cloud conditions prevented some targets from being bombed, the Fortresses did strike at Tutlow and Rostock in northeastern Germany and also at Leipzig, Oschlersleben, and Bernburg. More than 800 escorting fighters were in the air, and bomber losses fell accordingly. Most memorable about these missions was the fact that three Medals of Honor were awarded for deeds performed that day by Fortress crew members.

One of the B-17s that bombed Leipzig was flown by Lt. William R. Lawley of the 305th Bomb Group. His troubles began over the target when bombardier Lt. Harry G. Mason was unable to get the bombs to release. Then, just as they came off the bomb run, they were hit by fighters in a head-on attack. A 20mm shell exploded on the flight deck, killing the copilot instantly and wounding Lawley in the face. While fighting to pull the aircraft out of a dive after the copilot fell forward on the controls, Lawley saw that he had an engine on fire. With a full bomb load and a fire

Chow-Hound *was one of the better known Fortresses from the 322nd Bomb Squadron, 91st Bomb Group. It failed to return from a mission over France on August 8, 1944.* US-AAF

on board an explosion was imminent, so Lawler rang the bail-out bell.

It was then that Lawler learned that he had eight wounded men aboard, including himself. He managed to get the aircraft on an even keel and sent Mason back in the bomb bay to see what could be done about getting the bombs to drop. As both men worked desperately to remedy the situation they were again attacked by enemy fighters. Lawley managed to get the fire out in one engine and then the other while Mason managed to salvo the bombs. Although wounded, the gunners fought off the attack.

When Mason came out of the bomb bay he went back to his guns in the nose. After the fighters had been driven off, he went back to the flight deck where he found Lawley all but unconscious from the loss of blood. He immediately took over the controls and set the aircraft on course for England. It proved to be a long, slow flight on two engines, but Ma-

Previous page
Princess Elizabeth poses with the crew chief of Elizabeth's Own, *a B-17 named in her honor. The Fortress was assigned to the 423rd Bomb Squadron, 306th Bomb Group. 306th BG Assn.*

son made it. He spotted the small fighter field at Redhill and knew he would have to put down the Fortress there. He shook Lawley back to consciousness and Lawley took over. Through a supreme effort, Lawley managed to keep the aircraft under control, even though a third engine sputtered and died.

Ground crewmen service the oxygen system on one of the Fortresses of the 306th Bomb Group. 306th BG Assn.

Lawley told Mason to feather the propeller on the engine, and then on the final approach the last engine caught

fire. Miraculously, Lawley set down the aircraft as fire trucks and ambulances sped to the scene. Lawley was awarded the Medal of Honor and Mason the Silver Star.

Also in a 351st Bomb Group Fortress over Leipzig were navigator Lt. Walter E. Truemper and engineer-gunner Sgt. Archibald Mathies. A vicious fighter attack killed their copilot and gravely wounded their pilot. The bombardier hit the bail-out bell and went out the nose hatch, but most of the crew stayed aboard to see what had happened.

Truemper and Mathies managed to get the copilot's body out of his seat and the two of them took turns flying the aircraft. Although neither had any pilot training, they managed to bring the B-17 back to their home base where all of the crew bailed out except Truemper, Mathies, and their wounded pilot. The group commander told Truemper and Mathies to bail out but they refused to leave their skipper, who was still alive. Colonel Romig and Major Ledoux, tower officer of the day, took off in another B-17 and contacted Truemper on the radio. Twice they tried to talk the men through to a field landing, but failed. They then took them to Molesworth, but failed again. Finally, Colonel Romig decided to take them to a large field in the countryside. This time the approach was better but as they fought the controls, they came in nose-down and crashed. The aircraft burned, and all three men died in the crash. Truemper and Mathies were both awarded the Medal of Honor posthumously.

Overall, the losses for the Eighth Air Force were light for the number of aircraft that had been dispatched. Only thirteen B-17s were lost and the escorting fighters had done their job well, claiming sixty-one German fighters destroyed.

The following day, Eighth Air Force took advantage of the good weather and bombed Diepholz, Brunswick, and other targets of opportunity. The bombing at

Nine O Nine was one of the most famous B-17s with the 91st Bomb Group. It flew well over a hundred combat missions. Havelaar

Diepholz was successful, and Brunswick was bombed using PFF techniques. There was little Luftwaffe resistance and the Fortresses lost only twelve for the day.

Bombers were in the air for the third straight day by February 22, but the weather was so poor that the 3rd Division was prevented from forming up properly so they were recalled. The 1st Division formed up and went to Bernburg, where they bombed the Junkers factory.

The mission was costly to some groups, particularly the 306th Bomb Group which lost seven aircraft. The Luftwaffe took advantage of the bombers whenever the escort was not present. Although Mustangs saved them several times, the German fighters stayed away and as soon as they saw P-51s departing, they appeared. Twice, Lt. Col. Robert Riordan turned the formation into the attacking fighters, causing them to break off their attacks.

The 381st Bomb Group lost six aircraft on its mission to Bunde. Although there was now a fighter escort they, too, found that once there was any sort of a time gap when the fighters were not there, the Luftwaffe came in. They were greatly moved by the determination of the German fighters. When they got after one individual Fortress, the Germans would not let up until the B-17 went down. One of their B-17s had its tail section shot completely off.

The 1st Division lost thirty-eight B-17s, primarily to fighter attacks.

Weather caused the cancellation of missions on February 23, but the Fortresses were out in force again on February 24. This time, the primary targets were Schweinfurt and Rostock. The 1st Division put 238 B-17s over Schweinfurt, with good results. Only eleven B-17s were lost. On the 3rd Division's strikes at Rostock the bombing was largely effective and only five Fortresses were lost. It is possible that the primary reason the B-17s fared so well was that the 2nd Division B-24s took heavy losses from the Luftwaffe at Gotha, and the Fifteenth Air Force encountered heavy fighter opposition at Steyr, Austria, that same day.

The final day of Big Week, February 25, was not without its problems and losses. The 3rd Division struck Regensburg, and the 1st Division went to Augs-

The crew chief gives his aircraft, Miss Patricia, *of the 306th Bomb Group, a final once-over at the end of the day.* 306th BG Assn.

A nice formation of Fortresses from the 401st Bomb Squadron, 91st Bomb Group. Havelaar

Beautiful formation shot of 306th Bomb Group B-17s over England in 1945. 306th BG Assn.

burg. The 96th Bomb Group picked up high tail winds aloft and found itself over the target 40 minutes early. This caused them to miss the rendezvous with the escort, and the enemy fighters took advantage of the situation. The group lost four aircraft on the mission.

One of their B-17s that did come home made it the hard way. In a sudden blazing attack *The Saint* was hit by an Fw 190 that shot up the flight deck. The copilot was killed instantly, and the oxygen system was shot out. Lt. Stan Peterson, navigator, spent the next few hours going back and forth over the aircraft collecting walk-around bottles to keep the pilot going.

The 306th Bomb Group went to Augsburg to bomb the Messerschmitt Bf 410 plant on February 25. They encountered intense and accurate flak over Saarbrucken, which caused the formation to break while taking evasive action. This was the break the German fighters wanted. They dove to the attack and downed two Fortresses before they could close up the formation. A third B-17 was lost over the target to flak.

During Big Week, the Eighth Air Force lost ninety-seven B-17s. Coupled with the B-24 losses, the figure totaled 137. The Fifteenth Air Force, with B-17 and B-24 losses combined, lost eighty-nine aircraft. These American losses were quite high, but the Luftwaffe losses were also high. Their twin-engine units were all but wiped out by the escorting American fighters. Over 33 percent of the single-engine fighter force

was lost, taking with them 17.9 percent of the single-engine fighter pilots.

The damage to German aircraft plants was considerable as well. However, the Allies never seemed to realize how swift the recovery rate was in Germany. Through the use of slave labor, most damaged plants were back in production in a few weeks. Second, the enemy continued to scatter its production facilities over the countryside. Many small towns had factories turning out aircraft components. In truth, the manufacture of German single-engine fighters increased monthly almost up to the end of the war in Europe.

Ever since the US Army Air Forces began striking deep into Germany, all of the crews were on edge, wondering when they would be given the opportunity to strike at the heart of the Third Reich—Berlin. The order came down on

A 306th Bomb Group Fortress at rest on its hardstand. The 306th was one of the old-timers of the Eighth Air Force. 306th BG Assn.

March 3, but once the bombers formed up and headed out, they encountered weather that was so bad they had to turn back. A few struck targets of opportunity on their return.

Crews were briefed for Berlin again on the morning of March 4. More than 500 B-17s were dispatched. As they neared the enemy coast, most formations began to make 180 degree turns, heeding a recall to base. One formation continued to fly on toward Germany. The 95th Bomb Group, led by Lt. Col. Harry G. "Grif" Mumford, ignored the radio calls and continued to climb to get over the weather. Colonel Mumford and copilot Lt. Al Brown figured that if they aborted and returned on the same inbound route, they would probably be

mauled by enemy fighters, so they might as well take a chance on getting to the target.

The formation included 95th Group B-17s and a few from the 100th Group. The Fortresses climbed to 29,600ft to get above the clouds. They had not seen the ground since leaving England, but on reaching Magdeburg they began to get a few breaks in the clouds and were able to continue their run to the target through dead reckoning. Enemy flak was encountered and then a formation of Bf 109s was sighted. To the delight of the B-17s' crews, a formation of P-51 Mustangs came in to drive them off.

As the Fortresses approached Berlin, they began to encounter heavy flak. One shell came up through the B-17 being

flown by Lt. William Reis; it bored a 6in hole in the floor and then blew a 3ft hole in the top as it burst. It knocked one waist gunner back against the ball turret without hurting him, but it blew the other waist gunner completely out of the aircraft.

As the B-17s came down to the bomb run it was found that the bomb bay doors on the lead aircraft were frozen shut. In order for the formation to bomb, it was necessary to use the radar navigator on the Pathfinder aircraft to work

Note the short Cheyenne tail on this 306th Bomb Group B-17G. It gave the gunner more room and a new sight. 306th BG Assn.

in conjunction with Lt. Forrest Flagler, the bombardier in the lead ship. When the navigator on the Pathfinder aircraft told his bombardier, Lt. Marshall Thixton, to drop, Lieutenant Flagler fired a flare to tell the formation to let their bombs go. The bombs dropped on Berlin!

During their run, the bombers were attacked by enemy fighters and a few B-17s were damaged. As they turned westward and began their letdown, the B-17s took stock of events. Four 95th Group aircraft had fallen to the enemy, and the 100th Group had lost one. In all, twenty-one 95th Group and eight 100th Group B-17s made it through to Berlin.

On his return to base, Colonel Mumford did not know whether he would be court-martialed or rewarded for hitting the capital of Germany. When the Fortresses landed, a number of "big brass" and press awaited them. To Mumford's amazement he was decorated with the Silver Star, and Lt. Al Brown received the Distinguished Flying Cross from General LeMay in the briefing room.

The B-17s did not fly the following day, but on March 6, every bomber that could get in the air was sent to Berlin. This mission would prove to be the biggest air battle over Germany during World War II.

On the morning of March 6, 504 B-17s plus 226 B-24s escorted by 800 fighters set out to bomb Berlin. The 1st Air Division led the sixty-mile procession, followed by the 3rd Division with the

2nd Division bring up the rear. As the bombers thundered toward the target, the Luftwaffe Bf 109s and Fw 190s were assembling over Lake Steinhuder. The vanguard of the leading bombers had passed when Hauptman Rolf Hermichen led his Messerschmitt fighters to intercept. As he maneuvered his force into position, he noted that there were only eight escorting Thunderbolts to the front of the Fortress wing that he was closing on; the balance of the escorts in the area were to the south with the main bomber stream, which had flown off course.

The unfortunate wing that met the onslaught was the 13th Combat Wing composed of the 95th, 100th, and 390th Bomb Groups. The Fortresses of the 100th Group were led by Maj. Bucky Elton, who reported that they were vi-

A mixed formation of painted and unpainted B-17s from the 91st Bomb Group forms up over cloud cover. USAAF

B-17Gs from the 323rd Bomb Squadron, 91st Bomb Group. The aircraft in the foreground

failed to return from a mission to Nuremberg on November 2, 1944. USAAF

ciously attacked at 1159 hours by an overwhelming number of enemy fighters. They came in head-on through the 13th Wing.

After the first attack, Elton looked up and was stunned to see six of the high squadron's planes on fire in formation, long trails of fire streaming from their engines. When the fighters came back, all six of these aircraft fell out of formation. This attack took place over Haseluenne, a small German town northeast of Lingen.

In the first plane hit, both the pilot, Capt. David Miner, and copilot were killed in the initial pass and the nose was shot away. The balance of the crew bailed out as quickly as possible.

Lt. Zeb Kendall's aircraft exploded with all the crew lost, and Lt. Sherwin Barton and his crew bailed out of their flaming B-17. Lt. Dean Radtke's Fortress had two engines out and a fire in the bomb bay when his crew bailed out.

The fifth aircraft to fall from the high squadron was piloted by Lt. William Terry, and nicknamed *Terry and the Pirates*. Most of the controls were shot out and the aircraft went into a spin.

A 367th Bomb Squadron Fortress over England. The triangle denoted the 1st Bomb Division. 306th BG Assn.

This 398th Bomb Group Fortress apparently had a landing gear collapse when it came in. USAAF

Only three men were able to get out because of the centrifugal force of the spin.

Lt. Samuel Barrick in *Barricks Bag* had two engines out. Barrick salvoed his bomb load and managed to drop down out of formation and fly to Sweden, where the crew was interned.

In the low squadron, Lt. George Brannan had his right wing and two engines on fire when he ordered the crew to bail out.

Six men from Lt. Merril Rish's *Spirit of '44* bailed out when the entire aircraft became enveloped in flames. The fuselage broke in two at the radio room and threw two men out. The navigator was also blown out of a gaping hole.

Lt. Coy Montgomery was killed, but not before he managed to get his crew out. Also on fire was Lt. Robert Kopel's *Going Jessie*. Only three crew members survived.

The box of twenty B-17s was led by Capt. Jack Swartout, whose B-17 had collided with a Focke-Wulf 190 in the initial attack. Only a spar held on what was left of the rudder, but Swartout managed to get the aircraft down low and fly it back to England.

The lead was taken over by Lt. Edward Handorf, who managed to get the remnants of the formation over Berlin.

Unfortunately, Handorf's bomber was hit by fighters on the way home. A Bf 109 came in low from one o'clock and ripped the B-17 with 20mm fire. The wing tanks caught on fire, and only two men got out of the aircraft before it exploded.

Following the initial attack by fighters, Lt. John Lautenschlager's *Half and Half* developed a fire in the bomb bay. The bombs were salvoed and Lautenschlager proceeded to get his crew out of the aircraft before he trimmed it to fly without a pilot at the controls so he could bail out. He got out just before the Fortress exploded. All survived except the radio operator whose parachute failed to open.

Lt. Albert Ameiro's aircraft blew up shortly after the initial attack. One of the waist gunners was blown clear to become the only survivor.

Bigass Bird II fell with its tail on fire after the pilot, Lt. William Murray, was killed by 20mm from the fighter attack. Seven of his crew survived.

Lt. Celesta Harper had his oxygen system shot out and put his aircraft in a steep dive. He overstressed the aircraft, but managed to pull out and go home on the deck.

Lt. Mark Cope's aircraft was shot up badly but he, too, got down on the deck and scooted for home.

Lt. Frank Granack's aircraft was hit by flak over the target. This forced him out of formation and then the fighters came in. When they were through, he had only one good engine. With numbers three and four smoking, Granack trimmed up the aircraft and had his crew abandon the aircraft.

Thirty B-17s from the 100th Bomb Group had gone out from Thorpe Abbots that morning. Only half of them would return home, and of those aircraft that did survive, many were badly damaged.

A few minutes following the massive attack by single-engine fighters over Haseleunne, a second massive attack force was assembled. III/ZG 26 leader, Maj. Hans Kogler, assembled up a formation of so called "destroyer" aircraft composed of Messerschmitt Bf 110s and Bf 410s, all of which were carrying rockets. In the sky above them were seventy-two single-engine fighters which provided escort for the striking force.

At 1230 hours, Kogler got word from the group controllers to take his force from Magdeburg, where they had assembled, to intercept the lead groups of bombers, which was made up of the 1st and 94th Combat Wings. Just as the destroyer aircraft were positioned to attack they, in turn, were attacked by the escorting P-51 Mustangs. These fighters from the 4th and 357th Fighter Groups struck just as the Bf 110s began to fire their rockets from 1,000 yards behind the bomber stream.

At that moment the Bf 109s and Fw 190s of the destroyer escort force readied themselves to dive down to the rescue. However, the 354th Fighter Group, also in P-51s, arrived on the scene and climbed up into them. The destroyer formations were broken up by the Mustangs and many of the Bf 110s were shot down. Soon after, a massive dogfight began between the P-51s and the Bf 109s and Fw 190s of the destroyer escort force. The battle raged all over the sky while the B-17s plodded on to the target.

Eight Fortresses fell to the destroyer aircraft, and another three were destroyed in collisions caused by evasive-maneuver attempts to get out of the rockets' line of fire. Sixteen Bf 110s and Bf 410s were shot down, along with four P-51 Mustangs.

The 388th Bomb Group of the 45th Combat Wing was the last Fortress unit in the procession. The 388th had put up thirty-three aircraft for the mission to comprise an A Group, and the lead and low squadrons of a B Group, which was filled in by the 452nd Bomb Group.

As the 388th Group historian recorded: "Approximately 15 to 20 Fw 190s were first met on the route in to the target in the vicinity of Dummer Lake. The attacks, which started at 1200 hours, lasted until 1220 hours, were mainly directed at the groups ahead. No serious enemy attacks were again encountered until the formation was again in the same area on the return route. Here the same numbers of Fw 190s plus several Bf 109s pressed home vicious, daring attacks for 30 minutes. It was from these encounters that six of our aircraft were lost. The seventh was lost when one of our crippled ships collided with it. Attacks were from all clock positions but mainly from 10 to 2 o'clock high, with the enemy aircraft coming in line abreast and diving through the formation. Two to six enemy aircraft in line astern would also attack from the nose high. Crew members report that the 20mm cannon which were used exclusively fired both incendiary and time-delay shells. Many bombers shot down were observed to burst into flames immediately after the attacks by the enemy fighters.

"Inaccurate scattered flak was encountered from Amsterdam, Quakenbruck and Vechta. In the Berlin area an intense barrage was seen over the center of the city. Over the outskirts of the capital flak was continuous following, accurate and intense.

"Lt. B. K. Land's crew had several instances of conduct beyond the call of duty . . . Aircraft 9076 was flying number three position, lead element, low squadron, was violently attacked by enemy fighters at 1200 hours on the route to the target.

"In one attack by an Fw 190 the ship was racked by 20mm shells which knocked out an engine, damaged rudder and controls, hit oxygen lines, thereby forcing the plane to return alone. In this attack Sgt. Sartin was fatally wounded. The left waist gunner, Sgt. H. E. Kellner, was wounded but continued on his guns and is credited with destroying the attacker. The tail gunner, Sgt. C. S. Momeyer, was badly wounded in legs and face but continued at his guns while the attacks persisted and is credited with damaging an enemy aircraft in a later attack. He later crawled back to the

A Fortress from the 452nd Bomb Group begins its long earthward fall. USAAF

Two crewmen from a stricken B-17 free-fall before pulling their ripcords. USAAF

Rare view from the ball turret gunner's position. He saw everything looking up from his cramped, suspended quarters. USAAF

waist to assist the wounded waist gunner. Lt. Land brought the plane back safely, receiving excellent fighter escort until near the coast."

None of the three primary targets for the mission was hit effectively. Only the Genshagen aero engine plant was hit at all. The Erkner and Klein Machnow plants escaped completely. Very little damage was done to any military plants, and the most damaging effect was the fact that all industrial plants had to be shut down for several hours.

In the violent air battles, sixty-nine American bombers were felled along with eleven escorting fighters. This was far less than the 108 bombers and twenty fighters claimed by the Germans. By the same token, the bomber crews claimed ninety-seven enemy fighters while the escort claimed eighty-two. The total German loss was actually sixty-six aircraft.

As for the bomber crews, it had been a long mission, and the hell that many of them lived through that day would never be forgotten. For those most drastically affected, a post-mission event at Thorpe Abbots, home of the 100th Bomb Group, tells it best. Lt. Bob Shoens land-

ed his *Our Gal Sal,* which was one of the survivors of the 13th Wing's B Group that had lost ten of its fifteen B-17s. As he taxied to his hardstand, Shoens saw the squadron commander standing there waiting for them. "He was crying," Shoens said. "We were stunned to learn that we were the only aircraft of the squadron to return to the field and only one of four to make it back to England. What do you say, what do you do when your squadron commander is crying and wants to know what has happened? You do the same."

The bombers returned to Berlin on March 8. This time, the 45th Combat Wing was to lead, with the 96th Bomb Group in the forefront. The Luftwaffe had other plans for them. They attacked just as the 3rd Division was passing Hanover, and damaged the PFF aircraft to the extent that it was forced to abort.

The 96th Group was hard hit. When the PFF aircraft aborted, Lt. George Pond took over the lead. No sooner had he pulled into his new position when his aircraft was hit by oncoming fighters. The initial attack knocked out number two, three, and four engines, destroying most of the instrument panel and setting the aircraft on fire. Pond and his crew bailed out.

The second Fortress shot out of the formation was flown by Capt. Norman Thomas. After being badly damaged on

the first pass and forced out of formation, Thomas' B-17 was ganged up on by enemy fighters who didn't let up until the crew was forced to abandon the shot-up bomber.

Lt. Don Kasch was killed and his copilot broke his arm during the vicious attacks. Their aircraft went down on fire as crew members took to their parachutes.

A fourth B-17 was lost to fighters near Magdeburg, and a fifth B-17 was lost before they arrived at the initial point when its engine fire spread to the entire aircraft.

Lt. Clark Ross attempted to abort the mission after his B-17 had been badly damaged by fighters. The oxygen system and the intercom were out, so Ross dove down to a lower altitude for survival. However, fighter attacks continued, killing the bombardier and wounding the navigator in the face.

The copilot went back beyond the bomb bay to get the crew out of the aircraft. The two waist gunners were trying to help the badly wounded ball turret gunner out of his turret, and get a parachute on him. Hurriedly they jury-rigged the ripcord and pushed him out the fuselage door. Unfortunately, his parachute tangled with the horizontal stabilizer and then he fell.

After having attempted to help the ball turret crewman, the two waist gunners got to the door to bail out. As Sgt. Frank Ford stood in the door with his hand on the ripcord, he caught a blast of 20mm fire and was killed.

The 388th Bomb Group of the 45th Wing was also hard hit, losing five of their Fortresses to fighters. The Eighth Air Force lost a total of thirty-seven bombers on the mission, twenty-eight of them B-17s.

The B-17s went back to Berlin on March 9 and 22, suffering a minimum of losses while the Luftwaffe licked its wounds after losing 56.4 percent of its single-engine fighters and 22 percent of its single-engine pilots during the previous month.

The Fortresses took heavy losses again on April 11 when they journeyed out over the Baltic Sea to bomb targets in northern Germany. The primary target for the 3rd Division B-17s was Arnimswalde, but bad weather forced most of the Fortresses to hit Politz and Rostock. The 96th Bomb Group went to Ro-

stock, but was hit by large numbers of enemy fighters over the Baltic Sea and lost eleven B-17s.

Of their losses, two managed to ditch successfully, and survivors were picked up by the Germans. Another aircraft lost managed to make it to Sweden, where they received a fighter plane escort into the field and were interned.

On April 11, another member of the Eighth Air Force earned a Medal of Honor. This time it was a 305th Bomb Group pilot who would be honored for his ordeal in getting his Fortress back to England. Lt. Edward S. Michael piloted a Fortress named *Bertie Lee,* after his wife. Michael was a veteran with more than twenty-five missions to his credit.

Lieutenant Michael was part of a formation bound for Stettin loaded with incendiary bombs. Michael's bomber was the left aircraft in the high squadron element, a very exposed position.

The 305th had picked up some flak near Brunswick where *Bertie Lee* had received a pretty good hit in the wing. As they journeyed, they saw the Luftwaffe rip through a B-24 formation and then come back to hit the 305th Group northeast of Brunswick.

Two head-on passes by the Focke-Wulf 190s put four 20mm shells into the aircraft. One hit below the windshield and exploded in the cockpit. A fragment wounded Lieutenant Michael in the leg. This shell and another destroyed most of the instrument panel and severed the throttle controls to two of the engines, forcing the lieutenant to pull out of formation.

The radio operator then reported to Michael that the bomb bay was on fire. Michael told Lieutenant Leiber, the bombardier, to get rid of the bombs. He got no response and was not aware that Leiber's intercom was shot out. Lieu-

Smoke screen or no, the formation of B-17s heads on in to the target. USAAF

tenant Michael hit his salvo switch, but the bombs did not drop. Sergeant Phillips got out of the top turret, went into the bomb bay, and attempted to release the bombs, but they would not go.

The Fortress went into a spin and lost 3,000ft before Michael leveled out. The fighters came in again and did further damage. Phillips was already wounded, and the second attack knocked out his aircraft's chin turret. Lieutenant Leiber was firing away at the chin turret when an explosion knocked him back with the turret controls in his hands.

With many of the controls shot out, the bomb bay on fire with hung-up thermite bombs, and visibility all but nil from hydraulic fluid all over the wind-

85

A close-up of a 96th Bomb Group Fortress, a modified F model that has been fitted with a chin turret. USAAF

Bombs fall away from a Pathfinder aircraft of the 457th Bomb Group. Note the radar antenna suspended where the ball turret would be. USAAF

shield, Lieutenant Michael gave the bail-out order. Most of the crew bailed out.

As they let down with little visibility, Michael thought that he and copilot Lieutenant Westberg were the only crew aboard. They were down to about 2,500ft when Michael told Westberg to bail out. Each insisted that the other go first and when that got nowhere, Michael went back again to try to get the bombs out. When this failed, he returned to the cockpit and told Westberg they would have to go. As they dropped down to the nose hatch there sat the bombardier, Lieutenant Leiber. They told him to go, and he pointed to his parachute pack which was shredded by 20mm fragments. Michael offered Leiber his parachute, but he refused.

Lieutenant Michael went back to flying the aircraft manually and told Leiber to try the bombs again. He did, and by pulling and pulling he finally salvoed the bombs. Leiber then went back to the nose and fought off a fighter attack with the navigator's guns. Then they were hit by flak again and Michael dropped down to about 75ft, pulling up for houses and trees.

When they were finally out over the English Channel, Lieutenant Michael got the Fortress up to 3,000ft. Then another enemy fighter showed up and made passes from the rear where they had no guns. Michael turned and skidded to get out of the line of fire, and for no reason the fighter finally pulled off and went home.

Lieutenant Michael came in over the first landing field he could find and made a beautiful belly-landing. Weak from the loss of blood, Michael was taken to the hospital where he spent several weeks. He was awarded the Medal of Honor for his feat, and both Lieutenants Leiber and Westberg won Silver Stars.

On April 13, the B-17s experienced some of the heaviest fighter attacks that they had encountered for some weeks. The bombers went after targets at Schweinfurt and Augsburg. Thirty-two B-17s were lost. The 384th Bomb Group took the high losses with nine of their aircraft not returning.

Bombers were sent back to the Berlin area on April 18. The 94th Bomb Group was led by Maj. Lew Weimer, and Col. Charles Dougher was flying his first mission as 94th's commanding officer.

The weather was good until the Fortresses reached the target area. The 94th and the 385th Bomb Groups continued toward their targets, plowing through the weather. Most of the other bomb groups on the mission turned away from the bad weather and searched for targets of opportunity, and most of the escorting fighters followed. This gave the Luftwaffe the opportunity to come after the 94th Group which was without fighter protection. Some forty to seventy enemy fighters came roaring into the formation as a group, not as flights or in small numbers as they had been doing. The lead B-17 flown by Major Weimer was hit and fell out of formation shortly after they attacked. In the initial onslaught, eight bombers and two PFF aircraft were either shot down or fatally damaged.

As three of the crew members recalled, "We noticed a light brace of flak which diverted our attention and while so occupied, the fighters hit with a shocking suddenness." He went on: "They hit us in a bunch and then they were gone . . . the Luftwaffe appeared frantic and desperate without regard for caution. It seemed as if it was their last stand for survival."

The 94th Bomb Group lost eight B-17s while the entire B-17 force from the 1st and 3rd Divisions lost seventeen aircraft for the day.

The 306th Bomb Group had one of its worst days on April 24 when it flew in the low group of the B force bombing an aircraft assembly and repair center at Oberpfafenhofen, in southern Germany.

The unit lost its first B-17 shortly after crossing onto the Continent when Lt. Walter Peterson's aircraft was hit by flak. Number four engine was on fire when the Fortress pulled out of formation. Three chutes blossomed before the aircraft blew up.

Enemy fighters played cat and mouse for about an hour and a half before they decided to play the game in earnest. When they did come, the attacks were fierce and relentless. The demise of the 306th Fortresses occurred as follows: Captain Stolz's B-17 had three engines hit; Stolz salvoed the bombs and made it to Switzerland on two engines. Lieutenant Ebert's aircraft lost two engines and went to Switzerland. Lieutenant MacDowell was killed in the fighter attack; with number three

and four engines out, the copilot ordered the crew to bail out. Lieutenant Ramsey's B-17 lost two engines and had a fire going; the crew abandoned the aircraft. Lieutenant Tarr's aircraft was hit by fighters; Tarr ordered his crew to abandon aircraft, and it exploded after the crew had cleared the aircraft. Lieutenant Schwedok's B-17 lost two engines; he salvoed his bombs, and went to Switzerland. Lieutenant Coughlin's crew lost five men to the fighters before they hit the silk. Lieutenant Biggs' aircraft was on fire, and number three and four engines were shot out; the crew parachuted and the aircraft blew up. The last to go was Lieutenant James, who was checking out a new aircraft commander. The new pilot, Lieutenant Vander-Marliere, was wounded in the initial attack and was pinned against the aircraft when he first bailed out. He finally fell clear and the parachute opened successfully.

The 1st Bomb Division lost twenty-seven Fortresses, with the 306th Bomb Group absorbing ten of the losses.

The bomber crews of the Eighth Air Force regarded the 100th Bomb Group, which had become known as the "Bloody

The B-17G Milk Run Special. 306th BG Assn.

Hundredth," as the hard-luck group among them. By the middle of May, the aircrews from the 96th Bomb Group would argue the point. They lost six B-17s on March 8 at Berlin and then eleven at Rostock on April 11. Their mission to Brunswick on May 8 cost them ten Fortresses. Then on May 12, they went to Zwickou, Czechoslovakia, and lost a dozen aircraft when their wing was cut to pieces by the Luftwaffe.

Things did not get off normally for the 96th on May 8. Rather than use their usual eighteen-ship formation, Group commander Col. James Travis insisted on using a new fourteen-aircraft formation that he had come up with. The group was airborne in two sections, an A Group and a B Group.

The first thing that went wrong was when the lead PFF aircraft was forced to abort the mission because of troubles in the aircraft's oxygen system. Lt. John White took over the lead of the A Group in his PFF aircraft. Then a time foul-up ensued when the 96th Bomb Group ar-

A formation of Fortresses from the 381st Bomb Group with a P-51 Mustang for escort. USAAF

rived at its rendezvous too early and encountered a B-24 formation which forced the 96th north of their course. After the Liberators moved on, the 96th could never get itself into the bomber stream with the 3rd Division where it belonged.

German fighters attacked in the Dummer Lake area. Some thirty to forty single-engine fighters roared in, closing to near ramming, before they broke and went downward. Three of the 96th's B-17s went down on the first attack. Lt. Charles Birdsay's aircraft went down under a swarm of fighters. Lt. Harold Eye's B-17 lost its number two engine and had its left wing on fire when he gave the order to abandon ship. Two men bailed out before Eye decided to

crash-land the stricken plane; Eye and his copilot died in the crash. Lt. James Kirkpatrick's aircraft blew up. There was only one survivor.

Lt. George Sterler assumed the lead of A Group. Eight of his aircraft dropped their bombs on a B-24 outfit's PFF markers. On withdrawal, the 96th was hit once more in a furious encounter with a formation of Focke-Wulf 190s.

Lt. Harold Niswonger's aircraft was hit in the number three engine and a fire started. His copilot and radio operator were both wounded. Niswonger rang the bail-out bell, and then he and the engineer-gunner went back to help the radio operator. Niswonger's B-17 then exploded after being rammed by an Fw 190, which probably had a dead pilot at the controls.

Lt. John White, who had led the A Group to the target, had his Fortress riddled on the withdrawal attack and hit the bail-out bell after the aircraft burst

into flames. Some of the crew got out before the aircraft exploded.

Lt. George Sterler, who had led the B Group to the target, went down in flames as well. Also victims of the second attack were Capt. Milton Shoesmith who crash-landed and saved all his crew, and Lt. Frank King who lost his rudder and stabilizer, yet managed to crash-land his aircraft after five of his crew bailed out. This act saved a wounded man, but cost King a leg. The tenth Fortress to fall was flown by F/O Leo Green. All the crew bailed out except for the tail gunner, Sgt. Harry Shirley, who was still blazing away at the fighters even though he was seriously wounded in both feet. Shirley was blown out of the aircraft and survived to receive a postwar Distinguished Service Cross for his action.

A Fortress named *Reluctant Dragon*, flown by Lt. Jerry Musser, made it home to Snetterton that day. The aircraft was badly damaged, and one waist gunner had been killed. After six of the crew bailed out, Musser, along with the engineer, T/Sgt. Leon Sweatt, and the bombardier, Lt. John Flanyak, managed to bring the ship in to roost.

The crews of the 96th Bomb Group were still reeling from their losses on May 8 when they were briefed for what would be the first mission of the new campaign to destroy Germany's sources of energy. The Eighth Air Force dispatched nearly 900 bombers escorted by over 700 fighters to strike oil targets.

The 96th was assigned an oil plant at Zwickou, Czechoslovakia. Once more, fourteen-plane formations were used and twenty-six B-17s were dispatched. The mission went well until about noon, when a big gaggle of Bf 109s and Fw 190s, accompanied by a few Bf 410s, decided to concentrate on the 45th Wing. Before it was over, the men of the 96th and 452nd Groups would classify this mission as their Ploesti.

The German attacks were flown in three continuous sweeps. After making their passes, the enemy regrouped about 2,000 yards from the bomber formation and then came back in. Each assault lasted three to four minutes. A navigator's log from the 96th Group shows that the attacks came at 1210, 1224, and 1230 hours. After each pass, three or four fighters would linger to catch any cripples that fell out of formation.

On the first attack the leader and deputy leader of A Group were knocked out as well as the leader of B Group. Capt. James Knupp, A Group leader in the PFF aircraft, went down with his right wing cut off at number four engine and on fire. Col. Marcus Lemley, commander of the 339th Squadron, was aboard. Only Captain Knupp and the radio operator survived. The deputy leader of A Group, Capt. Jack Link, and all of his crew except for the navigator were lost.

Lt. Tom Moore flying the lead and PFF aircraft for B Group had six officers aboard. When the first attack transpired, the nose was blasted with 20mm fire. Moore and Lt. Richard Thompson were both killed. The regular copilot on the crew, Lt. Vic Johnson, flying the tail position, bailed out. There were no survivors in the nose of the aircraft.

The Fortresses flown by Lts. Robert Simmons, Robert Lewis, and Harold

The B-17G Toggle Tessie. 306th BG Assn.

Tucker all went down in flames. Lt. Herb Moore, flying a PFF aircraft, tried to take evasive action when another B-17 blew up, and Moore's B-17 collided with the B-17 flown by Lt. Art Hon. The bombardier and navigator on Moore's ship were killed, as were all the men in the nose of Hon's B-17.

Lt. Charles Filer had three engines shot out before he gave the bail-out order. The left wing of Lt. Wilford Kin-

man's aircraft started to burn, and his crew bailed out. Lt. Bob Laurie's aircraft was possibly hit by a falling Bf 109. Only two men survived.

Lt. Jerry Musser, who had nursed *Reluctant Dragon* home on May 8, didn't make it back from this mission. His navigator and radio operator were killed in the fighter attack, and the ship was damaged so severely that Musser crash-landed it in enemy territory. The rest of the crew survived, but Musser suffered a mangled hand in the crash.

The 96th Bomb Group suffered twelve losses, but the 452nd Bomb Group took fourteen losses in the fighter attacks. One of the 452nd Fortresses that made it back that day was flown by Lt. Milan "Mike" Maracek. As he recalled: "The Fortress over us exploded and a body of a crew member came tumbling and crashed into the nose of our ship. The force of the impact sheared off the glass nose, ripped out our nose guns, and the shattering glass threw our navigator and bombardier back five feet and threw them against the step going up to the cockpit. Both men were wounded. The navigator was hit in the stomach by flying metal and the bombardier received a gash over his eyes from a piece of flying glass.

"One Fw 190 raked the ship with bullets from the nose to the tail. A shell hit the top turret gunner in the side of his head and he died instantly. Bursting at the left waist window, another shell exploded and blasted the glass window and metal frame to pieces. A metal screw from the frame embedded itself in the gunner's nose. The right waist gunner received a wound over one of his eyes, the ball turret gunner was hit in the head, and the tail gunner was injured in the back."

Despite their wounds, the living gunners remained at their posts and kept scanning the skies for fighters. The radio operator, S/Sgt. Dwight Miller, went from one to the other administering first aid. Miller said he just tried to keep them conscious, although some were getting weak from the loss of blood.

The aircraft continued on the bomb run, then dropped its load and headed for home. The oxygen system was knocked out, so the crew took turns using a walk-around bottle. The bomb bay doors refused to close. With the nose shot out and the bomb bay doors open, the aircraft was not able to keep up with the others and had to leave formation. Maracek took the Fortress right down

A B-17G of the 96th Bomb Group at rest. An ever-alert ambulance sits in front—standard fare on airfields. Ethell

on the deck and hoped for the best. Two engines failed, and then a Bf 109 appeared. The left waist gunner gave the Messerschmitt a burst and the fighter departed.

The Fortress *Lady Stardust II* managed to avoid most of the flak along the coast, but when it reached the English Channel, it couldn't quite make it all the way home. The pilot ditched and the nine survivors were rescued from the sea.

Beginning in May 1944, the bombers of the Eighth Air Force began to fly numerous tactical missions to set the stage for the invasion of the Continent. These missions were directed at marshaling yards, bridges, and any sort of transportation target that would prevent the Germans from reinforcing their positions on the Normandy peninsula where the invasion would take place. Airfields were also prime targets. One thing that the bombers had accomplished was to drive the Luftwaffe from its bases in the occupied countries in order to defend the Reich. When invasion did come, there were few German fighters based in France.

On D-day, June 6, 1944, the bombers of the Eighth Air Force flew more than 1,700 sorties in support of the invasion. There were bombers continuously over tactical targets behind the beachheads. The greatest reward for the crew members was the fact that they were supporting the ground forces, and that losses to the bombers were minimal in these tactical strikes.

The most exciting event for the bomber crews of the Eighth Air Force after D-day was the first shuttle mission to Russia. The units were to take off from their English bases, bomb targets en route, and continue on to land at bases in Russia. From there they would bomb targets in the Balkans and land in Italy. From Italy they would bomb targets en route back to England.

Two bomb wings participated in the mission: the 13th Wing composed of the 95th, 100th, and 390th Bomb Groups, and the 45th Wing composed of the 96th, 388th, and 452nd. The planes flew the first leg of the mission on the morning of June 21, and they all bombed their tar-

The radio room and ball turret were wrecked on this Fortress, but it still came home. US-AAF

gets with good results. Then they continued on across Poland and into Russia.

The 13th Wing landed at Mirgorod while the 45th Wing landed at Poltava. There they were entertained by the Russians with food and drink. A good time was being enjoyed by all at Poltava when the air-raid alarm sounded. Unknown to the Americans, a German reconnaissance plane had followed the bomber stream to Poltava and flown back to report their landing ground. That night, two bomber units composed of Junkers Ju 88s came over, marked the field with flares, and began to bomb it. The Russians had few antiaircraft guns, so the Germans bombed for more than two hours as they devastated the bomber force on the ground.

When the survey was made the next day, two Americans had been killed and six wounded. Of the seventy-three B-17s on the field, forty-seven had been completely destroyed, two were good only for cannibalization, fifteen were repairable within seven days or more, and only nine were repairable within one day. American commanders were disgusted that they had been so poorly protected by the Russians, but all had the utmost praise for the common Russian soldiers, men and women who had done their utmost with their limited antiaircraft weapons to drive away the German bombers and later, to fight the many fires.

The remaining American aircraft on Russian bases were immediately disbursed and personnel were moved around. Repairable aircraft were worked on, and a task force was mounted to fly a mission en route to Italy. They finally took off on June 26, bombed an oil refinery at Drohabycz, Poland, and continued on to Italy.

The hundreds of Fortress crew members who were stranded in Russia had to be flown out by Air Transport Command. They were picked up from the Russian bases and sent back to England by way of Tehran, Cairo, Benghasi, and Casablanca.

The oil campaign continued throughout the summer of 1944. While the bombers of the Fifteenth Air Force out of Italy continued to strike at the main source of oil supply, the Romanian refineries at Ploesti, the Eighth Air Force bombed the synthetic oil refineries that were clustered primarily in central Ger-

Waist ripped wide open and ball turret is gone from this miraculously returned 351st Bomb Group B-17. USAAF

many. As the attacks continued, the buildup of antiaircraft defenses continued. Flak became a major factor in bomber survival as the flak batteries became more proficient and radar tracking enabled them to fire with great accuracy.

The 100th Bomb Group ran afoul of the flak batteries at the Leuna oil plant at Merseburg on July 29, 1944. As the A Group came in from the south, they ran into a barrage of extremely heavy flak. In the next few minutes, the low squadron of the lead group lost five out of six B-17s. The high squadron lost one aircraft to the barrage.

The B Group's lead aircraft, flown by Capt. Joe Zeller, was hit in the Tokyo tank just after bombs away. The aircraft burst into flames immediately, and the crew bailed out. A second Fortress in B Group was badly damaged and had to ditch in the North Sea. Fortunately, the crew was rescued by German ships.

All total, fifteen B-17s were downed over Merseburg that day, with the 100th Bomb Group losing eight aircraft.

One sighting that had been made on July 29 and a combat that ensued brought further evidence that the Luftwaffe was ready to put some new weapons into the air. An escorting fighter encountered a Messerschmitt Me 163, a rocket-powered interceptor capable of being launched from the ground and making brief, but very destructive attacks with 30mm cannons. The Me 163 encountered on July 29 was on a test flight. It was attacked by an American escort fighter, which put some telling hits into it before it screamed earthward.

Following the invasion of France, the bombers flew many tactical missions supplying Free French forces arms to combat the Germans behind the lines. One of these missions saw a copilot flying as a formation observer in the tail. Sometimes it got hot back there!

On July 14, 1944, Lt. C. B. Robbins, Jr., of the 385th Bomb Group, was flying the tail gunner's position on a mission to Valance, France. As Robbins told the story: "On this particular mission we were to lead the low group to take arms to the Free French in southern France. We were the lead ship, the group command officer took my seat and I, as copilot, was assigned to the tail as formation control target.

"This was my second trip to drop tubes of arms. I recalled what a beautiful sight [it was] to see the thousands of colored parachutes floating to the earth landing in open fields and the Free French running out to pick them up in their trucks and haul them away. I thought I would take some photographs of this wonder sight. However, about the time I was getting my camera out one of the waist gunners called over the intercom saying there were Bf 109s at about three o'clock coming down the bomber stream. As we had a lot of jovial comments about fighters, I replied, 'Let's cut all the crap, you guys, there is no such thing as fighters way down this far in southern France.' As I looked back over my shoulder, much to my surprise, there were Bf 109s coming down the bomber stream. They made a turn to the right and started to make a pass at our number six ship in the lead squadron.

"Naturally, I grabbed the twin .50 calibers in front of me and aimed at the first fighter, had it in my sights, and pulled the trigger. Nothing happened. I forgot to take the safety off.

"By the time the second ship came through, I was smart enough to take the safety off and fired at him. He was a good distance away, but at least I heard the rattle of guns.

"I took a shot at the third one, too, and missed, but I was really holding the trigger down. Then I noticed I had followed the Bf 109 down through our formation and was firing very close to one of the ships in our formation.

"Then another Bf 109 came through and by that time I had shot up all my ammunition or jammed the guns. Shows you how good a gunner I was. After the 109s, we went on in at tree-top level and dropped our parachutes and came on home. It was a total of about nine hours and thirty minutes on that flight.

"There was some discussion from one crew back at debriefing that they had checked their plane on the hardstand and it looked like they had received some hits from machine guns rather than from the 20mm of the 109s in their left wing, and they were wondering if anyone knew or saw any other fighters during the attack. Not to make confessions about my gunnery ability, I made no comments."

The threat that was most feared by the Eighth Air Force was the Messerschmitt Me 262. This was a new fighter powered by two jet engines that provided enough thrust to give it an 80–100 mph speed advantage over the P-51 Mustang. It was also heavily armed with 30mm cannons, and its fire on the bomber stream could be lethal. With its rate of closure, there was no way that the escorting fighters could stop its attacks. The only solution for the American fighters was to locate the bases of the jets and attack them on takeoff or landing when they were at a decided disadvantage.

The summer of 1944 saw two more shuttle missions to Russia by the B-17s. A force of seventy-six Fortresses escorted by Mustangs bombed the Focke-Wulf factory at Gdynia, Poland, en route to Russia on August 6. They flew one mission out of Russia and then departed for Italy on August 8. This time there was no air raid, and all went well for the American fliers.

The final shuttle to Russia began on September 11 when seventy-five Fortresses and their escort attacked an armament plant at Chemnitz en route to their bases in the east. They stayed a very short time, departing on September 13 en route to Italy on their way home.

On September 11, when one formation of B-17s had gone to Russia, the balance of the 3rd Division attacked other oil targets. The 100th Bomb Group was cruising along en route to Ruhland when, as the group historian recorded, "at 1205, unheralded and with no alarm on VHF, the Luftwaffe hit with everything it had, when three waves of enemy aircraft came deceptively from out of the sun to completely overwhelm the trailing and unprotected low group of the 100th C formation in a frontal attack, to tear the 350th Squadron apart and at the same time knock the six planes in the lead element out of formation."

Captain Giles, whose aircraft had its wing tips burning and breaking up, ordered his crew to bail out. Lt. Joseph Raine, who was flying on Giles' left wing, had his aircraft blow up; Raine and four of his crew were killed. Lt. Albert Trommer's B-17, flying Giles' right wing, was downed with only four survivors. Lt. Harold Taylor had been directly behind Giles; he did a wing-over with gas tanks afire, righted his aircraft, and tried to make a crash-landing—but all of the crew except the waist gunner were killed.

Two other Fortresses out of the same formation were hit and tried to make a run for home, but both were caught and shot down by fighters in their attempt.

The low element of C Group was also badly hit and lost three of its number quickly. Lt. Wesley Carlton's B-17 was hit, and only the navigator and copilot survived. Both of Carlton's wingmen also went down, with only seven survivors off the two crews.

Two Fortresses were shot out of the high element, making a total of eleven aircraft lost by the 100th Bomb Group in a very brief encounter. There was a twelfth aircraft lost on the mission. Lt. Raymond Heironimus' Fortress survived the first attack, but pulled up in a stall and spun down to 6,000ft. At that point the radio operator bailed out. The pilot set course for France and had hoped to make it to Paris, but finally had to set down in a turnip patch close to the front lines.

The following day, the Luftwaffe once more violently opposed missions against oil targets. The 306th Bomb Group was busy bombing Ruhland. The routing called for the 40th Bomb Wing, of which the 306th was a part, to fly to the north of Berlin, past the city defenses, and then turn south to Ruhland. As the Fortresses passed north of Berlin it

A 388th Bomb Group B-17G above England. The fact that the ball turret guns are pointed downward indicates the gunner is out of the turret, or just about to get in. Ethell

was noted that some of the formations ahead were turning too close to Berlin, and were getting in the flak there. The 306th lead got off to the left, hoping to miss the antiaircraft fire. Before they got clear, two Fortresses were hit. Lt. John W. Sasser, leading the high group, had two engines shot out immediately, so he lost altitude, with his group following him down.

The low group, which was trying to get out of the flak, nearly collided with another group that came barging in from their right and caused the formation to break up.

The 306th Bomb Group historian states: "At this moment about twenty-five Fw 190s jumped the disorganized planes. The entire attack did not last more than five or six minutes, but accounted for seven planes from the 306th Group, one of which crash-landed in England. The lead group of the 40th A Combat Wing which hung together solidly was not attacked and reports attacks on other groups as being from 5 to 7 o'clock high, level and low by enemy aircraft flying four to six abreast. The lead group lost one aircraft to flak.

"The low group reports that about twenty-five Fw 190s came from 11 o'clock high firing at the group to their left and made one pass, then turned and came at the low group from 6 o'clock low in five waves of three and four aircraft each. They half rolled beneath us and fell away steeply. The low group lost five aircraft to fighters, one of which crash-landed in England.

"The high group was attacked by seven to eight fighters and lost one to flak. Two planes of the high group tagged on to the lead, while the remaining planes of the high and low, with a few stragglers from the group which was responsible for breaking up the 40th A CW formation, struggled together into group formation and pulled clear as P-51s came to their rescue."

Maj. Robert Farwell had been leading the high squadron of the lead group when his aircraft was hit by flak. With a fire in the nose, he ordered his crew out. Lieutenant Sasser, who was leading the

96

high group when he was hit by flak, tried to get out and away, but was caught by enemy fighters and forced to crash-land. Only three of his crew survived the landing.

When the fighters came, Lt. Earl Barr's B-17 had two engines on fire when he ordered bail-out; Lt. Paul Bailey's B-17 had one engine on fire and another fire in the radio room before he ordered the crew to bail out; Lt. Lewis White had his aircraft shot to pieces and his tail gunner killed before the crew parachuted; Lt. Charles Wegener flying *Umbriago* had all his aircraft's controls shot out and an oxygen fire before he ordered his crew to bail out; *Belle of the Blue* with Lt. Daniel Gates at the controls was completely on fire in the rear when it went down; and the aircraft flown by Lt. Marvin Freeman was shot in two by the Focke-Wulfs.

The 351st Bomb Group was also hard hit on the mission, losing six of their Fortresses to Focke-Wulf 190s.

More than one thousand bombers were launched by the Eighth Air Force on September 28 to bomb oil targets in the Third Reich. One of the units en route to Magdeburg was the 457th Bomb Group. Since their entrance into combat in February 1944, the group's losses had been light and they had been lucky.

The group's luck ran out on September 28, however, when they were attacked by some fifty Bf 109s and Fw 190s just before their bombers turned on the initial point. The fighters came in low from four to nine o'clock, attacking the rear of the bombers. In a period of 12–13 minutes six aircraft were damaged badly enough to fall out of formation. From that point on, these six aircraft came under constant attack until they were abandoned by their crews. Two of the Fortresses were seen to explode.

As the Eighth Air Force moved into the fall of 1944 the numbers of B-17s increased. In the summer of 1944, it had been decided that the number of operational Fortresses would be increased. Over a period of two months or so, five B-24 units were converted to fly B-17s. The groups so changed were the 486th, 487th, 490th, 493rd, and finally the 34th, which became operational in B-17s on September 17, 1944. This gave the Eighth Air Force a total of twenty-six

Fortress groups, which meant that a maximum effort by the bombers could put more than 1,000 B-17s aloft!

Strikes at Berlin continued. Although many of the missions to the German capital no longer brought Luftwaffe attacks, there was always the possibility that it could happen. On October 6, the 385th Bomb Group suffered its highest loss of the war while flying a strike to Berlin. All eleven aircraft of the high squadron were shot down. The Luftwaffe amassed a formation of approximately seventy-five fighters, and sent them down in waves from five to seven o'clock high. By concentrating on the one unit, they managed to overwhelm the massed gun defenses of the bombers. Observers recall that in seconds the sky was marked with five B-17s exploding and five more smoking badly.

The following day, the bombers of the Eighth Air Force were out continuing their attacks on oil targets. The 94th Bomb Group's B Group was doing well until about 12 minutes before reaching the initial point. Suddenly fifty to sixty enemy fighters emerged out of high cloud cover. Single- and twin-engine attackers were scattered in disarray as they came in from the rear. In waves of eight and ten aircraft, they closed to attack. After firing at close range they split up, peeling off left and right with a few going under the formation and executing a split-ess.

The B-17 gunners fired for all they were worth In a very short period of time, the escorting fighters arrived, but it was too late. Nine aircraft were either missing or in the process of going down.

Most of the Fortresses that were hit either exploded or went down in flames. One B-17 had its whole tail section shot off. Lt. Julius Loesing and his copilot managed to regain control of their Fortress after it went down in a spin, and they crash-landed the battered bomber in a field. Once the dust settled, it was found that all the crew had survived except the waist gunner who apparently had been killed in the fighter attack.

Lt. R. E. Kennedy rang the bail-out bell on his Fortress when it was badly hit by the fighters. The aircraft was enveloped in smoke, and it began vibrating badly. Three of the crew bailed out immediately. Suddenly, the smoke cleared and Kennedy decided to see if he could

keep the aircraft flying. He managed to stay in the air long enough to reach a field in Belgium, where he landed safely.

While fighter attacks continued to be sporadic, there was no lack of flak. The 351st Bomb Group attacked the synthetic oil plant at Politz that day and lost seven of their B-17s to flak. The lead plane, flown by Lieutenant Colonel Glawe, left the formation with two engines feathered and a large hole and fuel leak in one wing and went to Sweden. Before the day was over Glawe and his crew would be joined by three other Fortresses crews from the 351st, whose aircraft had also suffered extensive flak damage.

Lt. Einer Peterson had headed for Sweden after losing an engine and having his fuel tanks holed. As he fell behind the formation, a second engine stopped because of lack of fuel. Then as Peterson's aircraft crossed Bornhalt Island in the Baltic Sea it was hit again by flak and lost a third engine. Peterson prepared to make a crash-landing in a field. As he got ready to set down, he sighted a number of people in front of him digging potatoes. He pulled up to avoid the potato pickers, which caused him to run out of room to land in the field. The B-17 smacked into a clump of trees, and only two of the gunners survived the crash.

The primary target on November 2, 1944, was the Merseburg-Leuna synthetic oil plant. Over 1,000 bombers were to strike at the target, and this was one day that the Luftwaffe put up its maximum force to intercept them. However, more than 900 American fighters were airborne to escort the bombers, so the Luftwaffe had to carefully select its point of interception.

The 91st Bomb Group lost one Fortress to an electrical fire before the initial point. Upon arrival over the target it was found to be socked in, so bombing was done by PFF. Flak was not heavy over the target. Just after the formation pulled off the target, it was hit from the rear by a bevy of Focke-Wulf 190s. They came in four abreast at six o'clock level and split-essed after making their passes.

The 91st lost ten aircraft to the Focke-Wulfs, two to flak, and one had to crash-land on its arrival in England.

The 457th Bomb Group, flying along with the 91st, was also hit by Fw 190s.

The severity of the combat was described by one of the gunners in the 457th: "The first two waves came in wiping out most of our box, but most of them were wiped out, too. The plane I was tracking and shooting at went over our tail and tore his left wing on the rear dorsal fin of our left wingman. I saw that our left wingman was also on fire behind his number three engine and just about then he peeled off and down. I swung my guns around to five o'clock again as the pilot, using evasive action, dropped the plane about twenty-five to fifty feet, leaving an Fw 190 shooting over us at a spot we had just vacated.

"The next plane that I fired at went over the top of us and straight down in front of our nose. At about that time Fw 190s were falling all around us as the third and final wave started to come in. They were more broken up than the first two waves because some of them were picking out stragglers as they fell out of formation.

"As I brought my guns back to six o'clock two more fighters were coming in close to our tail, one at five o'clock and the other directly on our tail somewhere under us. I could hear the ball turret gunner firing away. I started firing at the one at five o'clock, and the radio operator was firing at him, too. He started to smoke as he fell off to the right, and down under our belly he burst into flame. The other one lost his prop and blew up about twenty-five feet from our tail."

It is likely that the 91st and 457th Bomb Groups fell victim to the Focke-Wulf 190s from two assault groups of the Luftwaffe, IV/JG 3 and II//JG 4. With a total of sixty-one Fw 190s, they claimed some thirty B-17s around noon that fateful day. However, they lost thirty of their own aircraft, with seventeen pilots being killed and seven wounded.

A Fortress from the 447th Bomb Group with Lt. Robert E. Femoyer aboard as navigator was another aircraft that was severely damaged by flak on the mission to Merseburg. When the B-17 was damaged, Lieutenant Femoyer was severely wounded in the back and in the side by shrapnel. Although he was in extreme pain and weak from the loss of

A formation of B-17s forms up for a mission over England. Ethell

98

blood, he refused to take a shot of morphine. Femoyer refused any assistance, for he wanted to be able to navigate his crew home safely. He asked to be propped up on the floor where he worked with his charts and instruments until he directed his Fortress over the English Channel. Only then would he take the shot of morphine.

The aircraft made it back to England and to a safe landing. Femoyer was

removed from the B-17, but died shortly thereafter. He was posthumously awarded the Medal of Honor.

Two additional Medals of Honor were posthumously awarded to members of a Fortress crew for their performance on a mission to Saarbrucken, Germany, on November 9. Lt. Donald J. Gott was the pilot and Lt. William E. Metzger, Jr., was the copilot of a B-17 from the 452nd Bomb Group that was

Excellent photo of radar bombing by the 306th Bomb Group. Note the markers that the Pathfinder has just released to denote the target for the aircraft following. 306th BG Assn.

severely damaged by flak. Three of the engines had been damaged and number four was streaming fire as far back as the tail assembly. Some flares in the cockpit had ignited and with hydraulic

100

Naughty Nancy *graces the nose of a B-17G in England.* Ethell

fluid present a more severe fire was imminent.

The radio operator's arm had been severed below the elbow and the engineer-gunner was painfully wounded in the leg. A tourniquet was placed on the radio operator's arm. They had no static line to bail out the radio operator, so the two pilots conferred and decided to try to make it to Allied-held territory once the bombs were away. After dropping the bombs, they immediately set course for friendly territory. Upon arrival, Lieutenant Gott had Lieutenant Metzger see that the rest of the crew bailed out. Once this was accomplished, Metzger came back up to assist Gott in a crash-land-

ing. When they were only about 100ft in the air on their approach for landing, the Fortress exploded. All three men aboard were killed.

On New Year's Eve, 1944, the 100th Bomb Group set out to bomb Hamburg, Germany. The weather was beautiful, so rather than have the entire formation salvo on the lead bombardier, it was decided that each squadron would bomb individually. This concept proved tragic, however, for shortly after the initial point, the Fortresses were hit by swarms of Bf 109s and Fw 190s. The spacing out left them much more susceptible to enemy attack and the Luftwaffe took advantage of it.

A number of the Fortresses were hit by flak over the target and succumbed to these damages while others were damaged by flak and then came under attack

from fighters as they tried to flee for home. Two B-17s collided after leaving the enemy coast.

The majority of the enemy aircraft attacking the 100th Bomb Group were from II/JG 30, an assault group. All total, the 100th Group had twelve B-17s fail to return of which probably six fell to the fighters. Their attackers had eight pilots killed and three wounded.

The year 1945 saw the bombers of the Eighth Air Force reign supreme over Germany. They continued to strike at oil targets, communications installations, and airfields. The Luftwaffe got several jet units into operation, but never was able to have enough aircraft serviceable to really make a difference. The most successful unit was JG 7, which brought down a number of bombers during its career. Then in the spring of 1945 the select unit JV 44, commanded by the former chief of the German fighter forces, General Adolph Galland, got into combat. This unit was largely manned by Knights Cross winners who were very high scorers. Some of these aces got a number of victories flying the Me 262, yet the jet unit very seldom had over a half-dozen aircraft in service at one time.

In March 1945 Air Marshal Hermann Goering had organized the Sonderkommando Elbe group which was composed of volunteer pilots who would fly attacks in Bf 109s and press them to the point that they were committed to ram the bomber if they could not shoot it down. Both the Sonderkommando and the jets made a great effort on April 7, 1945, when the B-17s went after industrial targets in central Germany.

The intelligence report of 1st Air Division for that day states: "After a lapse of several weeks during which conventional single engine enemy aircraft have largely been non-active partners in the air war and even when encountered have shown little fighting spirit, today, in excellent flying conditions, the German Air Force put up a force of some 115–130 single engine enemy aircraft supplemented by more than fifty jets. From all reports it appears that this was a desperate attempt on the part of the enemy and although the enemy aircraft fought aggressively and made determined efforts to get through to the bombers, Allied losses were comparatively light while more than half the enemy force was destroyed or damaged. Signs of desperation are evidenced by the fact that enemy pilots deliberately rammed the bombers, bailing out before their planes went in the bomber formations and making fanatical attacks through a murderous hail of fire. Tactics were thrown to the wind and attacks were made from all positions, mainly in ones and twos. A few attempts were made to draw off fighter escort but the P-51s and P-47s were not fooled and did a good job of dispersing and destroying enemy aircraft.

"Reverting to this old policy of attacking in the area of Dummer and Steinhuder Lakes, the enemy met the leading groups of the first force at 1230 hours with some 105–120 Bf 109s, Fw 190s and 30 plus Me 262s flying between 18,000 and 30,000ft. Of these only some 45–50 single engine enemy aircraft and 15 jets managed to approach the bombers, destroying eleven. The B-17s claim 26 enemy fighters destroyed . . . "

One of the gunners that was successful that day was T/Sgt. Weaver L. Reckland of the 388th Bomb Group. Weaver related: "I got a Me 262 on the seventh and probably the only reason I shot it down was that the tail gunner had called to tell me a fighter was coming up fast on us from six o'clock. I was top turret gunner and we were under heavy fighter attack. I realized that unless he banked under us he'd have to come up in front of us. I turned my twin .50s around to one o'clock and waited a few seconds and sure enough he pulled up in front. He was in a steep climb at about one o'clock and not more than 300–400ft range. It was a dead straight shot and all I had to do was frame him in my sights and pull both triggers, keeping my turret tracking him on up until he trailed smoke. He spun into the ground without the pilot ever getting out. I didn't see the plane go but the copilot, ball turret, tail gunner, and waist gunner did and verified him for me."

On April 25, 1945, 307 B-17s were dispatched to Pilsen, Czechoslovakia, to bomb the Skoda armament plant. The bombs were aimed visually, and many strikes on the target were observed. Six B-17s were shot down by accurate flak. This marked the last combat mission of the B-17 Flying Fortresses of the Eighth Air Force. For thirty-two months, the famous aircraft had rained destruction over every possible target in northwestern Europe. With a force that had grown from the fledgling dozen B-17s that journeyed to Rouen, France, in 1942, it had culminated in a force of more than 1,000 Fortresses that dominated the daylight skies over Germany.

Chapter 7

North Africa and the Mediterranean

The 97th Bomb Group, pioneer bomber unit of the Eighth Air Force, became a pioneer in the new Twelfth Air Force in North Africa. They became involved early on when on October 19, 1942, Gen. Mark Clark and four of his staff climbed aboard a 97th B-17 flown by Maj. Paul Tibbetts, Jr. They flew to Gibraltar from whence General Clark and his colleagues made a secret mission to Algeria. Upon their return, they were flown back to England.

On October 29, six Fortress crews from the 97th flew to southern England for another top-secret mission. One waist gunner was dropped from each crew and was replaced by the crew chief. Baggage racks and seats were installed in the aircraft, while only the top turret, ball turret, and one nose gun received a small quantity of ammunition.

On the morning of November 5, 1942, the command staffs of the African invasion loaded aboard the 97th Bomb Group B-17s. Passengers were Gen. Dwight D. Eisenhower and his staff, Gen. Kenneth Anderson and his staff (to command the British First Army), and Gen. Mark Clark and his staff. Five B-17s took off in a heavy rain that morning for Gibraltar. One aircraft was delayed because of trouble with its hydraulic system. It departed two days later and near Cape Finisterre, the Fortress was attacked by three German fighters. Copilot Lt. Thomas Lohr was wounded and the

aircraft received minor damage. Aboard the B-17 was Gen. James E. Doolittle, new commander of the Twelfth Air Force.

Once the first landings were made in Operation Torch—the invasion of North Africa—on November 8, the 97th stood ready to bring the commanders into the theater. On November 9, General Clark and his staff were transported to Maison Blanche airfield at Algiers. General Doolittle took off in another B-17 destined for Oran. As the aircraft carrying General Clark was landing, a formation of twenty Junkers Ju 88s attacked the airfield. The Fortress turned off the end of the runway as bombs began to fall. One stick of bombs missed the B-17 by less than 100ft. Other B-17s en route to the airfield had to circle for an hour. The passengers all credited the American Spitfires in the area with defending the base and making their landings possible.

On the afternoon of November 16, the 97th Bomb Group under the command of Major Tibbetts led the first combat mission by B-17s in North Africa. The six Fortresses arrived over their target, Sidi Ahmed airdrome at Bizerte, Libya, and found it covered by clouds. They dropped down to 7,500ft and dropped their bombs on the hangar line. One B-17 suffered damage to its wing by intercepting fighters, but all returned safely.

Two more missions were flown by the 97th from Maison Blanche, both of them striking at El Aouina, outside of the city of Tunis, Tunisia. General Doolittle flew as an observer on one of the missions.

The Luftwaffe struck back on the nights of November 20 and 21. They made several runs across the airfield at Maison Blanche, dropping demolition and delayed-action bombs. The 97th lost a B-17 in each attack. It was decided that there were too many American aircraft on Maison Blanche, so the units were to be dispersed.

On November 22 the 97th Bomb Group was moved to Tafaraoui, seventeen miles southeast of Oran, Algeria. There they had a hard surfaced runway and several hangars. The base appeared to have great potential—until the rains came. There were no taxiways or hardstands for the bombers, so the aircraft sunk in the mud. Gasoline came in five-gallon cans, which made refueling the bombers a time-consuming chore because the B-17F carried over 2,200 gallons of fuel. The gasoline from the cans also had to be filtered through a chamois to remove water. Once the mud came and bombs were loaded, the wheels of the Fortresses sunk deeper and deeper in the muck.

The 301st Bomb Group joined the 97th at Tafaraoui in late November, and the two groups began to team up on

A Fortress of the 2nd Bomb Group, Twelfth Air Force, undergoing maintenance in North Africa. USAAF

their mission. Both groups went to Bizerte on November 28, and both experienced their first losses in North Africa. They were intercepted by Luftwaffe fighters that were very aggressive, and both groups lost two B-17s each. Lt. Robert Maher of the 301st Bomb Group made his bomb run on three engines. As he descended after the bomb run, his Fortress was pounced on by six Bf 109s that made constant attacks until the aircraft crashed into the sea and exploded. At the same time, four Bf 109s followed Capt. John Bruce off the target. Shortly thereafter, four parachutes emerged from the B-17, and it exploded.

In mid-December the 97th Bomb Group moved two squadrons to Maison Blanche and two to Biskra. The 301st Bomb Group also moved two of its squadrons to Biskra, but was forced to leave two at Tafaraoui. Regardless, the units operated under difficult conditions, and morale was low. Most of the fliers lived in tents, food was poor, and maintenance problems were legion. The engines and all operating parts on the aircraft were quickly eaten up by sand. Parts were hard to come by as well, for it seemed that B-17 units were on the end of the supply pipeline.

It had originally been planned that the Fortresses would be primarily strategic bombers. It did not work out that way in North Africa. They were constantly in demand as tactical bombers to strike at enemy troop and supply concentrations, airfields, and ports. B-17 units also continued to endure enemy air raids. Biskra was raided twice in January 1943, and some casualties were suffered.

The 97th participated in two missions against the French naval base at Ferryville, Libya, ten miles southeast of Bizerte, that were quite effective. On the first mission on January 8 they were intercepted by Luftwaffe fighters, but were able to put their bombs right on target. Five French vessels—a subma-

One of the most famous B-17 photos of the war. This Fortress from the 97th Bomb Group was ripped open by a Bf 109, yet it still made it home. USAAF

A P-38 tucks into formation with a Fortress from the 301st Bomb Group on the way home. The B-17 still has bomb bay doors open. USAAF

rine, a sailing vessel, a tug, an aircraft tender, and a patrol vessel—were destroyed or damaged beyond repair.

An attack on Bizerte in January was intercepted by fifteen Bf 109s, and the Fortress of Capt. Fred Dallas, Jr., seemed to get the most attention. A burst of flak had already knocked out the number two engine when the fighters came in. They immediately knocked out the communications system from the flight deck to the nose. The bomb bay doors were shot up, preventing them from closing, and the controls to the flaps were out.

Waist gunner Sgt. Elmer L. Burgher had been hit in the thigh by a piece of flak and he could only get up by pulling himself up on the gun as the occasion required. The ball turret was out of commission, and gunner Sgt. Edward Leary had been wounded in the left hand and shoulder.

The fighters began working on the Fortress and soon it became the center of their attention. Number three engine was hit and caught fire, but the fire was put out by diving the aircraft. Sergeant Leary now took over the waist gun from the wounded Sergeant Burgher. As the next attack came in from the rear, the tail gunner, the engineer, and radio operator all fired away but all took wounds from the fighter. The tail gunner was hit by a 20mm cannon shell, the radio operator got fragments in his knee, and a freak shot brushed the top turret gunner and severed the upright support of the turret, making it inoperative. On the same pass Captain Dallas was hit in the chest area by three machine gun bullets; all entered from the rear, went through his body, and struck the aircraft's instrument panel. Unbelievably, none touched a vital organ and he continued to fly the aircraft.

In the nose, the bombardier manned the guns while the navigator, Lt. Marvin Kay, worked to set a course that would take them to the Allied lines via the shortest route. With the Fortress down

El Diablo, *a veteran Flying Fortress of the 99th Bomb Group in Italy. USAAF*

105

This 99th Bomb Group aircraft is just coming in from a mission to France with number one engine still burning. USAAF

to about 1,000ft, Captain Dallas ordered all the crew except the copilot into the radio room for a crash-landing. With only one engine functioning properly, no flaps, bomb bay doors open, ball turret guns down, and wounded aboard, the pilot bounced the ship off a couple of sand dunes to slow his progress and then set the craft down in the sand. The tail section broke off and the copilot's elbow was dislocated, but all survived.

A mid-air collision on February 1 between a B-17 and a German fighter over the Tunis dock area became the subject of one of the most famous photographs of World War II. An enemy fighter attacking a 97th Bomb Group formation went out of control, probably with a wounded or dead pilot. It crashed into the lead aircraft of the flight, ripped a wing off the Fortress, and caused it to crash. The enemy fighter then continued its crashing descent into the rear of the fuselage of a Fortress named *All American*, piloted by Lt. Kendrick R. Bragg, of the 414th Bomb Squadron.

When it struck, the fighter broke apart, but left some pieces in the B-17. The left horizontal stabilizer of the Fortress and left elevator were completely torn away. The vertical fin and the rudder had been damaged, the fuselage had been cut approximately two-thirds through, the control cables were severed, and the electrical and oxygen systems were damaged. Although the tail swayed in the breeze, one elevator cable still worked, and the aircraft still flew—miraculously!

The aircraft was brought in for an emergency landing and when the ambulance pulled alongside, it was waved off for not a single member of the crew had been injured. No one could believe that the aircraft could still fly in such a condition. The Fortress sat placidly until three men climbed aboard through the door in the fuselage, at which time the rear collapsed. The rugged old bird had done its job.

The 301st Bomb Group was called upon to fly tactical missions on February 14 after the American ground forces had been routed by the Afrikakorps at Kasserine Pass. The 301st Bomb Group flew two missions the next day, one against an airfield and the second to strike at a German panzer division.

When the Fortresses arrived, the area was cloud covered. Most of the B-17s bombed to the east, but one squadron went down below 5,000ft to strike at the road along the pass. They destroyed a number of German tanks in the process.

In mid-February, the 97th Bomb Group moved to Chateaudun, Algeria, from which it would operate for quite some time. The 301st Bomb Group moved to its new base at Constantine, Algeria, on March 5. From their new bases, the two B-17s groups not only continued their tactical support of the US Army in North Africa, but they also began crossing the Mediterranean to bomb targets in Sicily, Sardinia, and Italy. The two bomb units that had become the 5th Bomb Wing in January were reinforced in March by the arrival of the new 99th Bomb Group.

The 301st Bomb Group ran into some sharp action on March 22 when they hit the docks at Palermo, Sicily. They were attacked by German fighters before they got to the target, but the enemy did little damage. As the 301st B-17s went over the target, the flak was accurate, but the Flying Fortresses dropped their bombs right on target. As they moved along after bombs away, the entire formation was rocked by a tremendous explosion. Their bombs had hit an ammunition ship.

As the 301st came off the target, they were hit by fighters once more. One Fortress had a fire going and Lt. James Hair's aircraft was hit in the fuel tanks. Fire immediately broke out, and his aircraft exploded at 19,000ft. Lt. Harbour Middleton's aircraft had been hard hit by fighters and knocked out of formation. Another Fortress then did a 360 degree circle and let down to protect him. This would later become a court-martial offense—to break formation to help a friend.

Middleton managed to limp in with his damaged aircraft, another example of excellence in B-17 design and construction. Two of the B-17's engines were out, but the amazing thing was that the fire from the fighters had severed the aircraft's right wing spar as well as its main longitudinal girder.

The 301st Bomb Group flew an outstanding mission on April 6. Thirty-three B-17s were airborne to attack a convoy fifteen miles off Bizerte, Tunisia. One aircraft aborted the mission, but the balance successfully dropped their bombs from 9,000 to 12,000ft. Those at the lower altitude met heavy flak and were attacked by twenty to thirty Bf 109s. Two Fortresses were heavily damaged and nine crew members were wounded. One of the wounded crewmen was responsible for the great success of the mission. Lt. Hyman Goldberg was hit by flak shortly before the bomb run. Although in great pain, he had a fellow crewman brace him so he could man his bombsight and release the bombs. His bomb run was highly successful: a 6,000–8,000-ton ship took a direct hit and blew up, and another vessel was left in flames. For the outstanding success of the entire mission, the 301st Bomb Group was awarded a Distinguished Unit Citation

The 301st and the 97th Bomb Groups teamed up on April 10 to attack two 10,000-ton Italian cruisers, the *Gorizia* and the *Trieste*, which were anchored at the port of La Maddalena, Sicily. Sixty B-17s set out to bomb the ships and hit them with 1,000lb bombs from 19,000ft. The 301st got twenty hits on the *Trieste*, and the ship quickly sank. The 97th Bomb Group got good hits on the *Gorizia*, but with its 9in armor, it was only damaged.

In April, the 5th Bomb Wing was joined by the 2nd Bomb Group which further increased the Flying Fortress strength in the Mediterranean. The 2nd Group would fly its first mission on May 3, 1943.

As the Allied ground forces forced the Afrikakorps to retreat into Tunisia, the Allied air forces cut off the German supplies coming from Sicily and Italy. The Fortresses continued to pound the ports, destroying the supplies that the enemy needed so badly.

Also targeted by the Fortresses were the airfields in Sicily, Sardinia, and Italy. On March 31 the 97th Bomb Group bombed Decimomannu and Nonserrato airfields in Sicily. In a 30 minute running battle with enemy fighters, the bomber crew claimed nine destroyed while no bombers were lost. More than one hundred enemy aircraft had been destroyed on the ground at Decimomannu. Gen. Carl Spaatz flew along on the mission as an observer.

The last African target was struck on May 5, when the Fortresses bombed the port of Tunis. German flak was still

strong, and a number of the B-17s were damaged. However, heavy damage was done to the docks, and eight small craft were sunk.

The bombing campaign against Sicily got under way on May 9, when 140 B-17s, making up the bulk of the attackers, bombed the docks at Palermo. Not only was the flak heavy and intense, but the bombers were attacked by a variety of fighters as they came off the target. No Fortresses were lost, but many of them came home with flak damage.

The B-17s nearly got Field Marshal Erwin Rommel on May 11, when they bombed Marsala, Sicily. Rommel was wounded and his aide was killed. A large number of German troops were also killed in the attack. Luftwaffe fighters intercepted the American bombers, and both the 2nd and 97th Bomb Groups lost two B-17s.

On May 25, strikes began against Messina, Sicily, on the eastern terminus of the island, which was only a few miles from the Italian mainland. Most of the flak guns that had been withdrawn from North Africa had set up at Messina, and it was the most heavily defended city in the Mediterranean at that time. It was later learned that on one of the bombing raids on Messina, the Italian cargo-carrying submarine *Romolo* was destroyed.

B-17s of the 97th Bomb Group in heavy flak. The vee formations of the Fifteenth were unlike those of the Eighth Air Force. USAAF

The Flying Fortresses were also striking at targets in Italy during this period. On May 28, a bombing mission to Leghorn sunk the Italian cruiser *Bari*. At the same time, the 99th Bomb Group hit an oil storage tank, which sent smoke rising to 10,000ft.

On June 5, the 5th Bomb Wing went after the remnants of the Italian fleet in the harbor at La Spezia, Italy. The battleships *Littorio* and *Roma* were both damaged, and the *Vittorio Veneto* was severely damaged. Although the flak was heavy and intense, none of the B-17s were shot down.

The 5th Bomb Wing continued to pound all the Axis airfields in the area in preparation for the invasion of Sicily. However, before the latter could be accomplished, the island of Pantelleria had to be neutralized. This small, rocky island was fortified with an airfield and some coastal guns that could be a real thorn in the side of an invasion fleet if they were not taken out. In the air efforts to knock Pantelleria out of the war, the B-17 groups flew 679 sorties and dropped 2,000 tons of bombs on the island. On June 11, the Italian comman-

This 2nd Bomb Group B-17 is undergoing some major repairs in North Africa. USAAF

der of the island surrendered. This was the first time that any objective had been conquered by air power alone.

The B-17s continued striking at airfields and coastal gun emplacements on Sicily up to the day of the invasion on July 10, 1943. Even after the invasion, the Fortresses continued to pound the dock installations at Messina. They also bombed numerous targets in Italy during July, the most notable being the city of Rome. The San Lorenzo marshaling yards were the targets in a city where the bombardiers had to be most cautious to avoid civilian and religious areas.

While the Fortresses continued to fly missions supporting ground forces in Sicily the big question that arose at the end of the Sicilian campaign was, why were the B-17s not used more at the straits of Messina where the German

Army left the island to retreat to Italy? Thousands of fighter and medium bomber sorties were flown through the flak-riddled skies over the area, but B-17s flew only 121 sorties while 100,000 German troops and 10,000 vehicles escaped.

With the fall of Sicily on August 11, 1943, the Fortress groups began systematic bombing of primarily transportation centers in Italy in preparation for the invasion of Italy. The city of Foggia, which in due time would become the hub of Fortress airfields, was a primary target in the attempt to stop all rail traffic to the south.

Foggia was bombed by the 5th Bomb Wing on August 19, 1943. Extensive damage was done to transportation facilities, and the electric power station was knocked out.

A very successful mission was flown against Luftwaffe bases around Foggia on August 25. One hundred fifty P-38 Lightnings took off and set course to the east toward Greece. The Fortresses then

took off and began to gain altitude. The American mission planners knew that the Germans had to be fully alerted to an attack and would be preparing for takeoff. As the Lightnings, which had dropped down to less than 500ft to avoid radar detection, neared the coast of Greece, they turned and headed westward. Coming in with the sun at their backs, the P-38s came in strafing at minimum altitude in three waves. Destruction and chaos reigned! As flames rose and pandemonium predominated, the Fortresses arrived and dropped their bombs. As a result of the mission at least forty-seven Luftwaffe aircraft were destroyed, many Luftwaffe pilots were killed or wounded, and a large number of ground installation targets were destroyed.

The bomber crews of the 5th Bomb Wing were aware that the invasion of Italy was imminent, particularly after they were briefed to bomb the headquarters of Field Marshal Albert Kesselring, the German commander in Italy, on the morning of September 8. One hundred and thirty B-17s bombed the headquarters at Frascati, a city east of Rome. The Luftwaffe rose to challenge the Fortresses, but the bombing caused great damage and the loss to the B-17 force was minimal.

Two hours after the bombers returned to their bases in North Africa it was confirmed that the US Fifth Army under the command of Gen. Mark Clark had invaded Italy at Salerno. Italy surrendered the same day, but the German forces fiercely defended the Italian peninsula.

The balance of the month of September 1943 saw the B-17s flying a number of tactical missions in support of the US Fifth Army. Bridges and troop concentrations were the primary targets. Heavy flak was still experienced around marshaling yards and other rail targets.

Several strategic missions were slated for the Fortresses in October, but most of them were not achieved because of bad weather. The bases in North Africa were mired in mud. When the bomber forces did get airborne, they experienced cloud-covered targets. The crews of the Mediterranean were not blessed with radar bombing aids, and their bombing attempts suffered.

Chapter 8

Fifteenth Air Force

On November 2, 1943, the four B-17 groups of the 5th Bomb Wing and two B-24 units of the Ninth Air Force were combined with two fighter groups from the Twelfth Air Force to form the new Fifteenth Air Force, which would become the strategic air force in the Mediterranean.

The new force wasted no time getting into action. On November 2, seventy-four B-17s and thirty-eight B-24s, escorted by seventy-two P-38s, set out on a 1,600-mile roundtrip to bomb the Messerschmitt factory at Wiener Neustadt, Austria. The Luftwaffe hit the first wave of bombers over the target with a force of eighty to one hundred fighters.

The second wave, composed of two B-17 groups, came in 45 minutes later. This formation was attacked by some forty-five enemy fighters. The concentrated attacks on the 301st Bomb Group cost them four B-17s. All went down in flames from the fury of the attacks, and all were from the 32nd Bomb Squadron. Two other B-17s were lost on the mission, but bombing results were good.

Two days later, ninety-five Fortresses set out to bomb the Bolzano Railroad Bridge. The formations encountered fighter attacks from some thirty-five to forty enemy fighters and lost five B-17s on the mission. Because of bad weather, only about one-third of the force bombed the bridge.

The rest of the month of November saw the Fortresses bomb targets in France, and a few missions were flown against tactical targets in Italy. The weather continued to be a big problem, and many aircraft had to abort most of their missions.

In December 1943, all of the Fortress groups moved from North Africa to Italy. Some of the moves were good; others resulted in mud problems that wouldn't be solved until January 1944.

A mission to attack the docks at Piraeus, Greece, on January 11 was marred by a tragic number of mid-air collisions. The weather was bad, limiting visibility to a few feet beyond the wing tips of the B-17s. The Fortresses of the 301st Bomb Group attempted to get some space between squadrons as they journeyed toward the target. At about that time, two B-17s from the 97th Bomb Group flew almost head-on into the 301st Group formation. One of them clipped the wing of the 301st leader's aircraft, apparently after having collided with another aircraft. One B-17 in the lead element exploded, as did two in the second element. Five B-17s from the 301st Group were lost as well as the two from the 97th Group.

The most miraculous escape was that of Sgt. James Raley, tail gunner on one of the affected aircraft. The tail was cut off Raley's B-17 in the collision and his tail section fluttered to earth, coming to rest in a clump of pine trees. Raley was not fully aware of what had happened until he opened his bulkhead door. Of the forty-seven 301st crew members who were in the planes that collided, ten survived. Eight of them evaded capture in Greece and returned to Italy.

Sgt. Thomas Huffman, waist gunner in one of the 97th Group B-17s that was involved in the collisions, managed to get his parachute pack snapped on as the aircraft broke up. The chute had just opened when it came to rest in a tree. He and two others were picked up by Greek underground partisans and taken back to Italy. They were the only survivors of the two 97th Bomb Group Fortresses.

The Fifteenth Air Force flew an extraordinary mission on January 30. Fifth Bomb Wing Fortress formations took off to bomb Luftwaffe fields in the Udine area of northern Italy. They knew they would be picked up on radar and that the German forces would be getting ready to intercept. Meanwhile, sixty P-47s of the 325th Fighter Group took off and sped northward on the deck, hoping to slip into the fight undetected.

The Thunderbolts got in the midst of the German fighters just as they were getting airborne and claimed thirty-six aircraft shot down for the loss of two P-47s. At that moment the Fortresses swept over the four German airfields and bombed them, destroying another

eighty aircraft on the ground. Their escorting P-38s shot down eight enemy fighters for the loss of a single P-38. All total, the Americans claimed the destruction of 142 Luftwaffe aircraft for the loss of five B-17s and three fighters.

The Fortresses also had to do quite a bit of tactical bombing during late January 1944 to support the American landing at the Anzio beachhead in Italy.

The B-17s of the 5th Bomb Wing flew their initial mission in the controversial bombing of Monte Cassino, Italy, on February 15. While ground-force leaders were of the opinion that the Germans were using the Benedictine Monastery as an observation post, its military value was debatable, and there was much discussion about whether it was really necessary to destroy such a valuable religious shrine. Nevertheless, early that morning, four B-17 groups put 142 aircraft in the air and dropped 354 tons of bombs on the monastery. It was deemed that the destruction was absolute, but such was not the case. Most of the treasured items survived, and the Germans continued to occupy the premises for another two months.

For several months, Allied planners had wanted to put into effect a plan code-named "Argument" that would bring about coordinated strikes against German fighter production. The Eighth and Fifteenth Air Forces would strike at the enemy's facilities by day and the RAF by night. Finally, planners were informed that beginning about February 19, the Continent should enjoy a few days of good weather.

As mentioned previously, these strikes in late February 1944 became known as Big Week. The RAF started things off on the night of February 19–20 when they struck targets at Leipzig, Germany. The following day the Eighth Air Force hit targets in the Leipzig area while the Fifteenth Air Force was scheduled to bomb Regensburg. Once more, weather got in the pic-

A 97th Bomb Group Fortress over the Alps. These mountains were always a hazard to the B-17s from Italy. USAAF

B-17 from the 342nd Bomb Squadron, 97th Bomb Group arrives in Russia on the first shuttle mission. USAAF

ture as the Fifteenth was forced to abort the mission. The most difficult obstacle for the Fifteenth in bombing Germany and Austria was getting over the Alps.

The Fifteenth got in on the act on February 22 when they got through to Regensburg. Liberators made up the first wave, and they absorbed the bulk of the Luftwaffe attacks. The Fortresses came in on the second wave, but only the

This 2nd Bomb Group Fortress came home with its radio room all but missing. USAAF

Welcome to Vienna. This target's defenses were second only to Berlin's. A Fifteenth Air Force Fortress challenges the barrage. US-AAF

97th and 301st Bomb Groups were able to bomb the primary target. Five Fortresses were lost on the mission.

On February 23, the B-17s were turned back because of weather, but all forces were up in strength the following day. The Fifteenth Air Force launched 151 Fortresses, along with 172 escorting fighters to attack the Daimler-Puch aircraft component plant at Steyr, Austria. Once more, weather got in the picture

and a number of the bombers were forced to abort. Rendezvous with the escorting fighters didn't come off either, and the Fortresses paid the price.

Only eighty-seven B-17s from three groups got through to Steyr and dropped 261 tons of bombs. More than one hundred German fighters intercepted the bombers. The 97th Bomb Group led the way to the target and dropped its bombs to good effect. The 2nd Bomb Group came under attack at 1215 hours at about twenty miles north-northwest of Fiume, Italy, and the attack continued for an hour. Then some P-38s arrived and the Luftwaffe left, but not before the 2nd had taken tremendous losses. Four-

teen of their B-17s fell to the attackers.

The 2nd Group historian recorded: "The attacks were made all around the clock, high, low and level and came in as close as fifty yards, singly, in pairs, four, six and eight at a time, using V-formations as well as abreast formations. Some of the twin-engine fighters stayed out of range and fired rockets, after which they came in for an attack, while other single engine fighters dropped aerial bombs. One group of fighters would attack, after which they would go out of range, re-form and come back in. In the meantime the other groups of fighters would be attacking, so there was a continuous attack on the bomber formation.

They picked on the second wave and literally picked them off like ducks. The only time the attacks let up at all was while the bombers were going through flak . . . Enemy pilots were experienced and aggressive."

The 429th Bomb Squadron of the 2nd Group was spared, probably because it was in the lead. The 20th Bomb Squadron lost two planes, the 49th Bomb Squadron lost seven, and the 96th Bomb Squadron lost five. The 97th Bomb Group got out unscathed and the

301st Bomb Group lost three Fortresses on the mission.

February 25 marked the last day of Big Week, and on that day the Fifteenth Air Force went back to Regensburg. The 2nd and 99th Bomb Groups led the Fortresses, followed by the 301st and the 97th Bomb Groups. The Fortresses had trouble with the weather from the time they formed up. The formations passed low over the Adriatic Sea, and enemy ships in the area reported their presence. Before the bombers reached

Crewmen have just exited a Fortress over the aircraft factory at Wiener Neustadt, a part of the Vienna, Austria, complex. USAAF

their target, they spotted the Luftwaffe force at seven o'clock. The enemy fighters immediately went after two straggling bombers, and then concentrated their fury on the 301st Bomb Group. Well over a hundred fighters began their attack near Fiume, Italy, and came in from astern in waves of up to twenty air-

A shiny Pathfinder aircraft of the Fifteenth Air Force releases its bombs on target. USAAF

craft. These fighters were responsible for all of the thirteen Fortresses lost by the 301st Bomb Group on the mission. Most of the unfortunate bombers were hit in the engines, starting fires from which a number of the aircraft exploded, or causing them to straggle from the formation where they were pounced upon and finished off.

One Fortress managed to make it back to Anzio beachhead, where it ditched just offshore. Another B-17 managed to make it home even though it had suffered an engine fire and other extensive damage in addition to having six of the crew bail out.

The 2nd Bomb Group, which had suffered such severe losses the previous day, had only been able to put up ten B-17s for the mission, but they struggled through even though they lost three of their number to German fighters.

This mission ended Big Week. There had been considerable damage done to the German fighter aircraft industry, but at most only a few weeks' production was lost. Perhaps the most damage was done to their existing fighter force. German records indicate that during Big Week, 198 single-engine fighters had been lost.

Weather continued to hinder Fifteenth Air Force bomber operations in March 1944, and most of the missions were tactical attacks against rail targets. The B-17s did fly a hotly opposed mission on the eighteenth of the month when they went after the airfields in the Udine area of northern Italy. Over forty enemy fighters came up to intercept the bombers, and they managed to down seven of the Fortresses. Assessment of the bombing indicated that at least fifty enemy aircraft had been destroyed on the ground.

The 5th Bomb Wing was reinforced in the spring of 1944 with the arrival of two additional B-17 groups: the 463rd and 483rd Bomb Groups. The 463rd Bomb Group flew its first mission on

Operations from Italian bases were very dusty and the steel-planking runways didn't help the situation. Here a B-17 from the 99th Bomb Group kicks up the dust. USAAF

March 30, 1944, and the 483rd Bomb Group flew its initial mission on April 12, 1944. This gave the 5th Bomb Wing a total of six groups with which to attack strategic targets.

The month of April saw a number of Fortresses bomb the ball-bearing plant at Steyr, Austria. Through an operations slip-up, the 97th Bomb Group lead aircraft pilot and group commander, Col. Frank Allen, flew the mission without a copilot. The mission was successful, but the 97th lost three B-17s in a running fight with enemy fighters. This mission also marked the first use by the Fifteenth Air Force of the tinfoil strips known as window to confuse enemy radar.

The mission to Gyor, Hungary, on

April 13 developed into a most unusual event for the 97th Bomb Group. Lt. Lawrence G. Moore returned from the mission alone, his crew having bailed out over enemy territory. It all began when a short circuit in the electrical system started a fire in the oxygen system. With smoke filling the aircraft and all the fire extinguishers expended, Moore assessed the situation and called for his crew to bail out. Ammunition was exploding and the men needed no urging. Moore had headed the aircraft back toward the Adriatic Sea and put it on autopilot after the last of his crew abandoned the B-17. When Moore dropped down by the nose hatch to depart, he saw the cause of the fire and pulled the oxygen line away from an arc of fire and

Sunny Italy and a 463rd Bomb Group Fortress at rest on its hardstand. Ethell

the flames subsided. Although his hands were severely burned, Moore went back up on the flight deck and began to run through the controls to see if the fire would continue to diminish. As the fire continued to wane, Moore settled down in the cockpit and headed out over the Adriatic, hoping no fighters would show up. From this point he only had one problem: he needed to transfer some fuel. So he put the Fortress back on autopilot, went back in the bomb bay, made the transfer, and went back to the cockpit to fly the aircraft in to Bari, Italy.

B-17 from the 97th Bomb Group showing considerable wing damage from flak. USAAF

At long last, the 5th Bomb Wing put radar bombing into effect on April 15. From the amount of oil smoke that penetrated the cloud cover over Ploesti, Romania, there could be no doubt that some of the oil refineries and storage facilities had been hit using the new Mickey aircraft.

A mission to Wiener Neustadt, Austria, on May 10 cost the 97th Bomb Group its commander, Col. Jacob E. Smart. The B-17 in which he was flying took a direct flak hit in the bomb bay and exploded. The loss of the lead aircraft on the bomb run caused a poor bombing pattern. Several other group Fortresses were seriously damaged, but no more were downed.

Also on the mission was the 463rd Bomb Group, which was attacked by forty to fifty German fighters just as it

came off the bomb run. There had been good fighter escort up to the initial point for the bomb run, but as they came off the run, there was no escort. The gunners of the new Fortress group put up quite a fight, but seven of their B-17s were shot down.

The 463rd Bomb Group was hard hit again on May 18, but not before they bombed their target. They were the only group from the 5th Bomb Wing that was not stopped by the weather that day, and they successfully bombed the Romano-Americano oil refinery at Ploesti using Pathfinder aircraft. Five minutes after bombing the target, about a hundred enemy fighters attacked and engaged the B-17s in a running fight for over 15 minutes before the P-38 escort arrived on the scene. Seven of the Fortresses fell victim to the Luftwaffe fighters.

During June 1944 the 301st Bomb Group tried its hand at AZON, or "Azimuth only," bombing. The AZON technique made use of radio-controlled 1,000lb bombs that could be steered in to the target—sort of a primitive version of today's "smart" bombs. The plane carried a radio control box, a radio receiver, and an antenna. The bombs were equipped with a set of ailerons on the tail fins, a gyro stabilizer, and a flare. A few seconds after the bomb dropped, a flare fired from the tail of the bomb, enabling the bombardier to follow it down. The gyros were designed to keep the bomb from rolling while the bombardier controlled the path of the bomb with a radio control box mounted next to the bomb sight.

Six aircraft and crews that had been trained in the use of the AZON bomb joined the 301st Bomb Group in April of 1944. These crews would fly a number of missions with the group from April through July, but the bombs were never as accurate as their designers hoped they would be. There were a few successes on bridges and viaducts, but not enough to warrant full-scale use of the weapon. It was finally decided that the weapon would work better from medium altitudes, so the program was turned over to B-25 units.

On the morning of June 2, 1944, three groups from the 5th Bomb Wing—the 2nd, the 97th, and the 99th—took off on their first shuttle mission to Russia. Flying in the lead 97th Group aircraft was Gen. Ira C. Eaker, commander of the Mediterranean Allied Air Forces. Lockheed Lightnings provided escort to the bombers that bombed Debreczen, Hungary, en route. No flak or fighters were experienced, but the ceiling continually decreased as the force flew eastward. By the time the Fortresses arrived at Poltava, Russia, rain was coming down steadily.

The Americans were treated royally by the Russians during their stay at

This 463rd Bomb Group B-17 lost its entire nose to flak over the target, but continued to fly for a short while before going down. USAAF

Poltava. General Eaker was rushed off to Moscow to report on the mission, but his men couldn't have been treated better. There was ample food and drink, and the Russians even put on a couple of musical shows for the aviators.

On the morning of June 11, the Americans took off on their return to Italy. More than one hundred B-17s bombed the airfield at Facsani near Bucharest, Romania, where a number of enemy aircraft were destroyed on the ground. One 97th Bomb Group B-17 was lost to enemy fighters when it lost an engine and couldn't keep up with the formation.

As summer continued, the primary target for the Fifteenth Air Force was the oil refinery complex at Ploesti, Romania. Defenses for the area constantly increased. By the end of the campaign against the complex, it possessed 558 guns and more than 2,000 smoke generators that were capable of covering the entire area in less than 40 minutes.

The raid on Ploesti of June 23 included all six groups of B-17s from the 5th Bomb Wing. The defenses were put into action promptly. Forty-plus single-engine fighters hit the Fortress formation before they arrived at the target area. When the bombers did get to the complex, it was covered with smoke and the flak barrage was hot and heavy.

A 97th Bomb Group Fortress flown by Lt. Edwin O. Anderson took a direct

A 2nd Bomb Group B-17 gets airborne in Foggia, Italy. Ethell

hit in the right wing while on the bomb run, shattering the control surfaces and ripping a fuel tank loose. The bomb run was completed with one engine out. As the B-17 emerged from the flak, it was immediately pounced on by enemy fighters. The tail gunner, Sgt. Michael J. Sullivan, was wounded by a 20mm shell that ripped through his position.

Sullivan's intercom was out, so he crawled up to the waist where the gunners picked him up and took him into the radio room. There Lt. David R. Kingsley, the bombardier, administered

first aid. As Sullivan recalled: "I was pretty banged up, and my chute harness was ripped off by 20mm cannon shells, and as I was in a daze and shocked, I couldn't see what was going on in the ship. I crawled out of the tail after I was hit. My waist gunners gave me first aid but couldn't stop the flow of blood that was coming from my right shoulder. They called up Lieutenant Kingsley and he gave me a tourniquet to stop the flow of blood.

"Finally the blood was stopped, but I was pretty weak. So then Kingsley saw that my parachute harness was ripped, so he took his off and put it on me. As I was laying in the radio room, he told me that everything was going to be all right

as we had two P-51s escorting us back to our base. We were still about 500 miles from home and the ship was pretty badly shot up. Finally, our escorts, the P-51s, were running low on fuel, so they told our pilot that they would have to leave and asked if we could make it. Our pilot thought he could and they left.

"As soon as they were gone, we were then attacked by eight Bf 109s who came out of the sun and started making passes at us. Finally, after about a fifteen-minute fight, we were told by the pilot to get ready to bail out as our ship was pretty well shaking apart in the air and most of our guns were knocked out. You see, that was the third group of enemy fighters to hit us that day.

"As soon as the bail-out bell was given, the rest of the gunners bailed out. Lieutenant Kingsley then took me in his arms and struggled to the bomb bay where he told me to keep my hand on the ripcord and said to pull it when I was clear of the ship. Then he told me to bail out. I watched the ground go by for a few seconds and then I jumped. Before I jumped, I looked up at him and the look he had on his face was firm and solemn. He must have known what was coming because there was no fear in his eyes at all. That was the last time I saw Kingsley, standing in the bomb bay."

Kingsley ran into copilot Lieutenant Symons as he went forward in the bomb bay. He asked where the pilot was, and went forward to the flight deck. As Symons bailed out he almost hit Lieutenant Anderson, who had just bailed out the nose hatch. Perhaps Kingsley was searching for a spare parachute that should have been aboard. The men parachuting downward then noted the weird maneuvers of their Fortress. Anderson thinks that Kingsley did his best to try to crash-land the B-17, but with only one engine going it proved to be too much for him. At last, it corkscrewed into the earth.

For his self-sacrifice, Lieutenant Kingsley was posthumously awarded the Medal of Honor.

The 5th Bomb Wing attacked Memmingen airdrome on July 18, 1944. Because of bad weather forty-four B-17s aborted the mission and twenty-seven

A head-on view of Fortresses outbound from their Italian bases to bomb a target in the Balkans. USAAF

others hit a railroad bridge in Italy on the way home. Only seventy-nine Fortresses hit the primary target. The 483rd Bomb Group arrived at Memmingen alone and went on to bomb the airdrome there, which was a center of jet fighter production. An overpowering force of some 125 German fighters attacked them while the fighter escort had to take on another 100. In a 20 minute fight all the way to the initial point, fourteen 483rd Fortresses were shot down. The remaining twelve went on to bomb the target.

B-17s from the 483rd Bomb Group with gear down for landing return from another mission over the Balkans. USAAF

Two shiny Fortresses from the 99th Bomb Group over the snow-capped Alps. The mountain beauty disguised a mighty obstacle that the bombers had to challenge. USAAF

The 5th Bomb Wing went after the aircraft factory at Wiener Neudorf on July 26, and everything went wrong for the 301st Group. For some reason, the fighter escort didn't make the rendezvous, but seventy-five to one hundred enemy fighters showed up prior to the initial point. The enemy continued to attack even while the Fortresses were on the bomb run. As they came off the run, the B-17s encountered a huge cloud that only served to spread the formation. As the bombers broke out of the cloud, the fighters hit again. The 301st lost eleven B-17s in the fight.

Most of the Fortresses went down in flames, and there was one mid-air collision. Of the 109 crew members who went down that day, forty-six survived.

The Fifteenth Air Force shifted its mission emphasis on August 12 to preparing for the invasion of southern France. On that day it sent all of its heavy bombers to strike gun positions. On the following day, another strike was mounted. The invasion came on August 15, and the 5th Bomb Wing was assigned targets along the beach between the Toulon and Cannes.

A very successful mission was flown to Ploesti on August 18. The target was the Romano-Americano refinery. The German defenders put their smoke generators to work, and it was originally thought that the target would be covered. The wind shifted, however, and the smoke dissipated, allowing the 97th Bomb Group, which led the mission, to hit the target dead center. Only three B-17s were lost on the mission, but the

B-17s from the 97th Bomb Group on the way to strike marshaling yards at Linz, Austria. Most welcome is the presence of the contrailing P-38s above them. USAAF

A B-17 from the 483rd Bomb Group goes down in flames over the target in Yugoslavia. USAAF

bombers left oil smoke towering up above 15,000ft.

August 19 marked the last mission to Ploesti. Soviet forces occupied the area on August 22. From April 5 through August 19, the 5th Bomb Wing hit Ploesti a total of fifteen times. The Fortresses flew 1,774 effective sorties against the targets there and lost forty-five B-17s.

The 2nd Bomb Group had a rough mission to Morovaka, Czechoslovakia, on August 29. The Luftwaffe caught their formation when the escort was not there and downed nine of the Fortresses. The entire 20th Bomb Squadron went down on this raid.

The 5th Wing went to Blechhammer North at Gleiwitz, Germany, oil refineries on September 13, and the 97th Bomb Group received its highest loss for one day when heavy, intense flak hit the lead aircraft at bombs away: Five Fortresses were lost and one was so badly damaged that it had to land on the island of Vis off the coast of Yugoslavia on the way home. Altogether, ten B-17s fell to the very accurate Blechhammer flak batteries.

In October, the 5th Bomb Wing started sending out "lone wolf" missions. These consisted of small numbers of aircraft for night raids on various strategic targets. These Pathfinder radar-equipped Fortresses primarily were to serve as nuisance raiders more than anything else. They kept the enemy flak forces at their posts, and kept civilians in air raid shelters through a great portion of the night. During 627 bomber sorties by the Fifteenth Air Force to the end of the war, seventeen bombers were lost, which was a rather high percentage, particularly for the damage they did. Very few sorties of this type were flown in 1945.

Bad winter weather took its toll of mission days during January and February 1945. Most of the missions that were flown during this period were tactical strikes in Italy. The strategic missions got going again in March with missions to Austria, Germany, and Hungary. A mission to Ruhland, Germany, got a heated response from the Luftwaffe, which cost the 483rd Bomb Group six B-17s.

On March 24, 1945, the 5th Bomb Wing went all the way to Berlin. One hundred sixty-nine B-17s, escorted by 289 fighters, made the long trip, and the Fortresses dropped their bombs on the Daimler-Benz tank works. A number of Messerschmitt Me 262 jets were seen on the mission, and one Fortress fell to the guns of a jet. All total, nine B-17s did not return from the mission, which ran over nine hours.

The Third Reich was on its last legs, and Allied air power dominated the German skies. By April, the B-17s of the 5th Bomb Wing had just about run out of targets. The majority of their strikes were tactical missions to northern Italy in support of ground troops.

The Fifteenth Air Force—an outfit that the Eighth Air Force had called "minor leaguers"—had done a "major league job" on the targets in southern Europe. The Fifteenth made great strides in knocking out Axis oil production by their attacks on the Ploesti complex, as well as the attacks on Blechhammer and other synthetic-oil targets. The aircraft factories of Regensburg and Vienna felt the full fury of their bombs while targets such as Budapest, Munich, and Brux were also on the Fifteenth's strike list. Additionally, they had a big job to perform in doing the tactical bombing of many targets in Italy, France, and in the Mediterranean as a whole. Regardless of the task, the B-17 Flying Fortress had done its job as well in the south as it had in flying from England.

Chapter 9

Shot Down–A Personal Remembrance

"Time to go." The most dreaded words that could come to a bomber crew member were spoken in the darkness of an Italian morning. It meant that I had to crawl out from under mosquito netting and join my fellow gunners sitting on the edge of the folding cots that graced our pyramidal tent home. An early morning cigarette was ritual before we gathered our flying gear from under the cots and stumbled along toward the lights that marked the entrance to the mess kitchen.

Once we had picked over the "rubberized" pancakes with the watery ersatz syrup and downed a welcome, warm cup of coffee, we went out to board the trucks that would take us down to the group headquarters area for briefing. We were still relatively new members of the 340th Bomb Squadron of the 97th Bomb Group. We had only joined this historic unit in early August 1944, but we had really flown our rear off in the few weeks since arrival. My first two missions had been to the oil refineries at Ploesti, Romania, so I knew that we definitely were in for no picnic in this theater of operations.

As we sat and squirmed in the smoke-filled briefing room, we anxiously stared at the covered map on the platform, wondering what our destination would be. A loud "Ten-Hut!" brought the room to attention, and "At ease" brought thuds of bodies dropping their rears back on the noisy steel stools that once had been a part of bomb cases.

The Fifteenth Air Force was in the midst of an oil campaign, so it was not surprising that when the cover was pulled from the map, the long red cord stretched near its limit to come to rest far up in the northeastern quadrant. "Men, your target for today is the Blechhammer South synthetic oil refinery near Gleiwitz, Germany," stated our group commander, Col. Nils Ohman. "This is another important oil target, and it is imperative that we knock it out." Further briefing went over routes, weather, possible enemy fighters, and I recall something more clearly having to do with "intense and accurate flak."

Following briefing, we boarded the truck once more and were taken to the equipment shack where we picked up our heated suits and parachutes. I recall being most chagrined over the fact that my nice, new parachute pack for my chest harness was not given to me. Instead, I was given a pack that was rather dirty and showed signs of abuse. Instead of arguing with the man behind the counter, I figured what the heck, I won't need it anyway. Little did I know!

We then trucked out to our individual aircraft. We were once again deposited on the hardstand of a shiny B-17G known only by the last three digits of its serial number "166." We did not have assigned aircraft in our unit; we

flew in whatever aircraft was assigned to us. However, we had been trying to get a mission in on 166 for two days prior to this September 13, 1944, meeting. On September 11 we got off in it. Once we were airborne, our assigned copilot became quite ill, and we were forced to bring him back to base. The following day we reported to 166, only to have the mission canceled because of bad weather over the target area.

On this particular morning, all seemed to be going well. I wiped down and checked out my waist gun, plus one of the cheek guns and one of the chin turret guns in the nose. Other little chores were taken care of, and there was time for a last smoke before we boarded the aircraft for taxying. Engines were started, and one by one the Fortresses in the area began to pull out on the steel taxi strips and begin the procession of roaring engines and screeching brakes as they maneuvered toward the end of the runway.

As we moved along, suddenly there was a blowing of a horn alongside, and we noted the operations officer in his jeep was signaling us to stop. As we braked to a stop, a man jumped from the jeep and ran to the waist door. We opened the door and let him in. He told our radio operator to go with the operations officer. Our radio operator had been reassigned to the lead aircraft at the last moment, and we were brought

The author's crew just before departing Drew Field, Florida, for Italy. Their fates in combat are in parentheses. Front row, from left: Lt. Bruce Knoblock, pilot (POW); Lt. Glen Tiffany, co-pilot (completed combat tour); Lt. Lee Cooning, navigator (POW with another crew); Lt. W. "Ted" Hill, bombardier (KIA with an- *other crew). Back row, from left: Sgt. Olis Henley, tail gunner (POW); Sgt. V. D. Smith, radio operator (KIA with another crew); Sgt. Roy McFaddin, ball turret gunner (POW); Sgt. Walter Brand, engineer-gunner (POW); Sgt. William Hess, waist gunner (POW). Not in photo: Sgt. Charles Collar, waist gunner (POW).*

The telegram that was sent to the author's father when he was missing in action.

the radio operator from the spare aircraft. This last-minute switch was to cost our radio operator his life.

Once we were airborne, we began to jockey for position in the formation. We were flying deputy lead in the squadron, which put us on the leader's right wing. We began our long climb to altitude and headed out over the Adriatic Sea. At 12,000ft, we went on oxygen and tested our guns. I pulled the charging handle a couple of times and triggered a short burst aimed down at the sea. The aircraft vibrated as the various guns were fired and the smell of gun powder permeated the air.

The trip to Blechhammer was a long one, and once over enemy territory, our visual sweep of the skies became more intense. After a time I sighted contrails high above us. As they came closer, I could recognize the silhouettes of P-51 Mustangs, our escort. There was certainly nothing more beautiful to bomber crew members than the essing flight maneuvers of four "Little Friends" against a beautiful blue sky. I often wondered how such a beautiful setting could preface a scene of death and destruction.

After a time, the contrails of our Little Friends turned away and we knew that we must be about to reach the initial point of our bomb run. As the aircraft in our formation maneuvered into position for bombing, I heard someone over the intercom say, "Target dead ahead. Damn, look at that flak." I turned off the power to my heated suit so all available electrical current could go to the bombsight and associated circuits. Although it was probably forty degrees below zero outside, sweat always seemed to pop out and my mouth became very dry. I snapped on my quilted steel flak vest, plopped the steel flak helmet down on top of my flying helmet, and set my eyes on the lead aircraft as its bomb bay opened. As soon as the lead plane dropped its bombs ours would go, too.

The flak was there, very intense and right in on us. It seemed that we were in a cloud of black puffs that were drawing closer all the time. There was a sinister beauty in these explosions against the sky—until you knew what they could do. Tensely, I glued my eyes to the lead ship and thought, it has to be any second now. Wham! "What the hell?" I cried out, and felt myself falling. The next moment, I found myself on the floor and

FIFTEENTH AIR FORCE
Office of the Commanding General
A. P. O 520

19 October 1944

Mr. Cas G. Hess
Box 638
Laurel, Mississippi

Dear Mr. Hess:

I regret to inform you that Sergeant William N. Hess, 18210045, has been missing in action since September 13, 1944, when the B-17 on which he was an aerial gunner failed to return from a daylight bombing mission to Blechhammer, Germany.

After successfully reaching the target intense and accurate anti-aircraft fire was encountered the result of which disabled Bill's aircraft. Only two parachutes emerged from the descending bomber. I sincerely hope that Bill was able to bail out. You may be sure that if additional information about him is received it will be forwarded to you promptly by The Adjutant General, Washington, D. C.

Bill has done a commendable job while he was with this air force. In recognition of his capable participation in operational flights he has been awarded the Air Medal. His many friends here wish me to extend deep sympathy to his family at this time.

Very sincerely yours,

N. F. Twining

N. F. TWINING
Major General, USA
Commanding

The letter that always followed up the missing status from the Fifteenth Air Force commanding general.

Fortress from 340th Bomb Squadron, 97th Bomb Group. USAAF

heard a hissing noise somewhere above me. Had we blown up? I was in a daze and everything seemed smoky or foggy. Slowly, I pulled myself up.

I looked at my side of the waist, which was a shambles; the plexiglass was gone, above the window was a large hole that a man could stick his head through, and two more holes were in the armor plate below the window. All around the window were a score of holes through the aluminum skin. Then as I looked above, I saw that the hissing was

coming from an oxygen line that had been shot out. My steel helmet was on the floor with a dent in it big enough for my fist, and as I looked down in front of me, some of the steel plates from the flak vest fell on the floor. The canvas holding it together was shredded.

I looked out the window, and the scene was one of devastation. There were still black blotches of flak everywhere. The wing of a B-17 fluttered down with both propellers still turning. Several parachutes drifted down through the flak and debris. Then I looked at our wing and got a real sinking feeling in the pit of my stomach. The number one engine had taken a direct

hit. The propeller looked as if it had been in a crash-landing, with all three blades bent back. The number two engine had taken a hit in the oil tank and the wing was covered with oil. The wing, itself, was full of holes and fuel streamed back in a white vapor.

We started to make big circles in the sky, losing altitude. The other waist gunner looked at me in dismay. He later told me that he looked at me on the waist floor and wouldn't look back, for he knew I had to be dead. The ball turret gunner was out of his turret and the tail gunner came forward. The latter reported that we had a hit in the tail and apparently some of the control cables were ripped apart in the rear. Our skipper, Lt. Bruce Knoblock, desperately tried to set a course south for Romania, which had just been overrun by the Russians, but he didn't have the controls to do so.

Then came the words "you walk back from this one." The copilot was sent back to see that the rear of the aircraft was cleared. One by one, the gunners went out the fuselage door. They told me to snap on my pack and bail out. Still in a daze, I went over and sat down on it. They got me up and in the door. I looked down at my ankles and then I was out. Don't know if I jumped or was pushed, but I have always figured the latter was probably true.

There was one thing about it: there was no sensation of falling. I remember seeing the aircraft going away from me and I pulled the ripcord. What a shock. As I swung under the canopy, I began to think, this isn't really so bad. Then, the risers popped up on me, hitting me under the chin, and I thought I had fallen out of the harness. Now, that was scary.

As I swung down, I began to see people running around on the ground. Then, TWANG! Hell, somebody was shooting at me. I looked and saw the parachutes of my other crew members now and noted where my friend, the engineer-gunner Sgt. Walter Brand, was coming down and planned to try to join him. Then all of a sudden the ground seemed to be coming up fast, and I was

falling right into a tree. I went crashing down the side of a large tree, taking off several limbs on one side before my canopy caught in the tree. I wound up like a kid in a swing, with my heels barely touching the ground. I couldn't have planned such an easy landing.

I got out of the harness, took off my flying boots, and put on my GI shoes, which I always tied on my harness ring. I was in a small patch of woods, so I got down in a ditch and covered my Mae West life preserver and my boots under some leaves. Cautiously moving in the woods, I came to a sudden stop when I heard a terrific roar. As I looked up I saw two Focke-Wulf 190s roar overhead. They were out looking for us in our crippled B-17. As I moved along once more, I heard TWANG! I was still getting shot at. I hugged the bottom of a ditch and moved along cautiously. Finally, I came to a road. Across it was about 100 yards of open field, but beyond that was a virtual forest. If I had been able to get into the forest , perhaps I could have evaded.

I waited a few minutes in a ditch alongside the road and decided I would make a run for it. Warily, I stepped out on the road and when I was about halfway across I heard TWANG! TWANG! I looked to my right and there, just coming around a bend in the road from the patch of woods that I had left, came three German soldiers, two with rifles and one with a machine pistol. For me, the war was over.

When these pictures were made at gunnery school, they jokingly were referred to as "MIA photos." Many of them became just that. USAAF

Chapter 10

Prisoner of War–A Personal Remembrance

Stalag Luft IV, where over 9,000 aerial gunners from the Eighth and Fifteenth Air Forces were held.

Following my capture by German troops, I learned more of the fate of my crew and the final status of our aircraft. I was taken to a cluster of buildings that housed the German headquarters of some sort of armored unit. When I was taken into one of offices, I was heartened to see the majority of my crew sitting there on the floor. The navigator who had been flying with us that day was quietly bleeding on the floor. He had been shot through the armpit coming down in his parachute. The Germans claimed that they thought we were Russian paratroops coming down!

That night we were taken to a German air base in Krakow, Poland. There we spent three days up on the third story of a building overlooking the airfield.

It was quite unusual to observe enemy Messerschmitt 109s and Focke-Wulf 190s leaving the field early in the morning to fly to advanced bases on the Eastern Front and then to return late in the evening. Somehow, the word must have gotten out about us, for many Poles came by our building late in the afternoon and would gaze up at us sitting in the windows and nod their heads.

The nine of us and four guards were taken down to the station one afternoon and put on a train going west. For several days we went across Germany, made a few changes, and observed many cities that had been heavily bombed. The one scare that we had was during a train change one afternoon. We were out on the platform with our guards when a German officer who was minus a leg came down to stare at us, and then the civilians began to stare at us. I got behind the big guard with the machine pistol and stayed there.

We arrived in Frankfurt, Germany, late one night and walked to Dulag Luft, which we were to learn was interrogation center for Allied aviators. There we were placed in solitary confinement cells that contained a cot and a stool and nothing else. I was so worn out that I slept the entire first day that I was there. It was only on the second day that I began to wonder if I would spend the rest of the war in the cell. We were given ersatz coffee in the morning and some black bread and margarine during the day, and that was about it.

Finally, on the third day, I was taken before the interrogator. When I told him only my name, rank, and serial number, he pulled out a large folder with 97th Bomb Group on the cover and began to tell me much more about the unit than I knew. He then wanted to know what a German boy like me was doing bombing the Fatherland. They had really hit the jackpot with the crew that I went down with; we had Hess, Knoblock, Wagge, Anderson, Brand (shortened from Brandt), and Henley.

Following that day, I was put in a regular stockade and reunited with my crew. The next day, we boarded a train that took us to another Dulag Luft, a transit camp. There we received a small POW kit that contained socks, underwear, toilet articles, and so on, which came through the Red Cross. We also got our first decent meal since capture.

Right after the meal, however, the air raid alarm sounded and Wetzler, the city near the camp, was bombed.

Late that afternoon, we enlisted men were gathered up for shipment out to a permanent camp. We bid our skipper good-by, and were taken down the road to Wetzler. Because of the bombing that day, we had a double guard, but the civilians were busy cleaning up and putting out the fires that were still burning. Rocks and curses came our way, and we had our first experience at being treated as "Luft Gangsters" and "Terror Fliegers." We were put in box cars, about thirty men on one end and four guards on the other, and told that we would be leaving that night. Meanwhile, rocks continued to bounce off the sides of the cars.

Our journey lasted four days and five nights, and we prayed for rain. Even though our cars were marked "POW" on the top, we were right behind the engine, and the balance of the train was made up of cars full of munitions going to the Eastern Front. We had the rails bombed out in front of us once, but fortunately ran into no strafing Allied fighters. Thank the Lord, he did let it rain on us most of the journey.

We traveled to Pomerania, in northeast Germany, and were unloaded at Grosstychow and taken to Stalag Luft IV. When we arrived, we were assembled before the headquarters building. When I looked up on the flagpole and saw the Nazi banner, the full realization came to me that I was a prisoner of the Third Reich. There was no mama, no papa, no Uncle Sam that was going to look after me in this place. From that day forward, the sight of the United States' "Old Glory" has had a special meaning for me.

Our stockade was not ready, so we were scattered in various barracks in A Lager. The room that I was placed in was filled with some of the oldest RAF prisoners in Germany. They were primarily sergeant pilots who had been shot down very early in the war. Before they came to Luft IV they had been in Luft VI, which was near Danzig. Here were men that had never seen a B-17 or B-24, from which most of the American POWs had exited.

After about a week or so, we were placed in the new stockade, C Lager. The barracks were large, prefabricated,

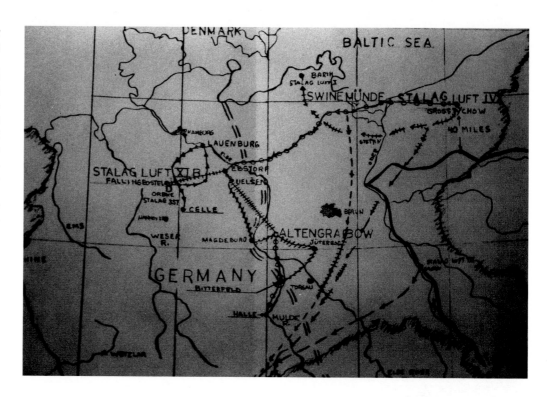

The top route, from Stalag Luft IV to Stalag XIB, was that followed by the author during his incarceration. O'Donnell

and not very well put together. We had about thirty men in each room and initially had no stove for heat and no bunks. We were issued one GI wool blanket and one German blanket. We had to team up with a partner to make a mattress consisting of the two German blankets stuffed with straw. We got no stove until the snow began to fly, and we got the bunks shortly before we had to evacuate the camp. Our German ration consisted of a bowl of kohlrabi soup at noon and a few boiled potatoes in the evening. These rations were supplemented by Red Cross parcels that were designed for a parcel a man per week. We got half parcels when I arrived at Luft IV, and this diminished to quarter parcels before we departed.

With little to do in the camp, we got to know our roommates real well. We soon knew their life histories, their ambitions, and their likes and dislikes. With the low-calorie diet, there was unbelievably little talk of females. The favorite pastime was listing menus of food the men wanted on their return home. All food was priced in cigarettes which were received in the Red Cross parcels. Most of us got about two packs a week.

The most exciting event we had in our room happened on a dark and cold winter evening. We had to place heavy wood blinds over the windows before

dark for blackout purposes. That night, one of our blinds blew off and the guard in the tower opened fire with his machine gun through the window. How thirty of us got through the door so quickly I'll never know. Miraculously, no one got hit.

On February 6, 1945, we were told to get our meager belongings together because we were being moved. The Russians were close enough that we could hear the artillery, and we had hopes of imminent liberation. Early that morning we were marched out to the front of the camp and given a Red Cross parcel each. Then we began a march that would be nothing but a trek of misery, starvation, and sickness. More than 8,000 men started out; some of them would not make it to the day of liberation, and many of them would suffer the throes of frostbite and dysentery before the end of the road.

We traveled northward to the port of Stettin, and I will never forget crossing the bay at Swinemunde and seeing a German U-boat coming in from the Baltic Sea with all the crew aligned on the deck. German Marines were busy

An older and hopefully wiser author after his return from POW camp.

building fortifications, and the whole area was a mass of activity.

Some days later, I had my little pack of possessions stolen and this left me with no changes of underwear or socks. Walking in snow and mud kept my feet wet. With the cold at night, it was not long before I fell victim to frostbite. This, coupled with a severe case of dysentery, made life miserable. I struggled along with a "sick party" who were often hauled in wagons pulled by oxen. How wonderful it would have been to be walking instead of freezing in the wagons!

At one point, those of us in the sick party were reunited with the marching columns and all were placed in box cars, about sixty to seventy men in each car. Most of the men were sick, practically all suffering from dysentery, possessing all but no food. We were transported to God knows where, and denied water or the opportunity to get out of the cars at any time. With only a box for dysentery, the air was stifling. It was reported that some of the men died during these four days, but I never knew of the deaths.

A number of men escaped during the days on the march, but this was extremely dangerous. All Germany was an armed camp and anyone caught without proper papers in any area would be shot at once. Many German soldiers were deserting, and this made the situation worse. Any of them who were caught were executed on the spot. It was reported and later confirmed that Hitler issued an order for all Allied aviator prisoners of war to be executed. Fortunately, cooler and more frightened heads in the Luftwaffe prevailed and the order was never seriously considered.

In late March 1945 our sick party was placed in Stalag XIB, an international camp at Falling Bostel, Germany, which was about fifty miles north of Hanover. There we had an assortment of prisoners from every country imaginable. The majority of the men that we were placed in the stockade with were British paratroops who had been captured following the fiasco at Arnhem, Holland.

Liberation finally came on April 16, 1945, when the British 7th Armored Division "Desert Rats" overran our area. There were only about 300 fellow Americans in the camp, but we had a wonderful time celebrating our freedom with the men from many nations.

I was flown to Brussels, Belgium, and then returned to American control at Namur, Belgium. We traveled to Camp Lucky Strike at Le Havre, France, from which we departed for the United States.

Chapter 11

Postwar

Regrettably, most B-17s went to the desert at Davis-Monthan Field in Tucson, Arizona, or other installations where World War II aircraft went to await the cutter's torch. Fortunately, there were some that were purchased and were to see long lives in various uses. The US Army Air Force and the later US Air Force used some of the B-17s in air-sea rescue service. These aircraft carried large rescue boats mounted on the belly of the aircraft so they could be dropped to maritime-disaster victims.

In civilian service, a few were converted to private corporate transports, but more were used as mapping aircraft or fire bombers. Quite a number of Fortresses were active in firefighting activities up until the 1970s.

At this late date, just about all of the surviving B-17s are museum items, some static and some still flying. There are a number of beautifully restored Fortresses still flying on the air show circuit.

Texas Raiders *is the B-17G that is the pride and joy of the Confederate Air Force. It is on the air show circuit annually.* R. Gill

Thunderbird *belongs to the Lone Star Air Museum located in Galveston, Texas, and is one of the most beautifully restored B-17s around.*

Sentimental Journey *belongs to the Arizona Wing of the Confederate Air Force and is beautifully restored.*

An air-sea rescue RB-17 at Nisawa, Japan, in 1949. Thompson

Memphis Belle *undergoing repairs in Memphis, Tennessee, in 1986.* Thompson

Static-display B-17G at Eighth Air Force Museum, Barksdale Air Force Base, Louisiana. Bardwell

The pride of the Arizona Wing at rest at its home base. The aircraft is widely known on the air show circuit.

Thunderbird *from the Lone Star Air Museum features the markings of a historic Fortress from the 303rd Bomb Group.*

Texas Raiders *taxis in following another successful air show.*

Appendix I

B-17 Specifications

Designation	No. Built	Wingspan	Length	Height	Engines	Top Speed	Cruise	Range
Model 299	1	103'9"	68'9"	15'	P&W 750hp	236mph	140mph	3,011mi
Y1B-17	13	103'9"	68'9"	15'	WR-1820	239mph	175mph	2,430mi
Y1B-17A	1	103'9"	68'9"	15'	WR-1820	271mph	183mph	-
B-17B	39	103'9"	67'10"	15'	WR-1820	286mph	-	3,000mi
B-17C	38	103'9"	67'10"	15'	WR-1820	300mph	227mph	3,400mi
B-17D	42	103'9"	67'10"	15'4"	WR-1820	318mph	-	2,540mi
B-17E	512	103'9"	73'9"	15'4"	WR-1820	-	226mph	3,300mi
B-17F	3,405	103'9"	74'9"	19'2"	WR-1820	325mph	160mph	4,420mi
B-17G	8,680	103'9"	74'4"	19'2"	WR-1820	302mph	160mph	3,750mi

Appendix II

B-17 Flying Fortress Serial Numbers

Y1B-17	36-149 thru 36-161	B-17F-DL	42-2964 thru 42-3482
Y1B-17A	37-369	B-17F-VE	42-5705 thru 42-6204
B-17B	38-211 thru 38-223	B-17G-BO	42-31032 thru 42-32116
	38-258 thru 38-270		42-97058 thru 42-91407
	38-583 and 38-584		42-102379 thru 42-102978
	38-610		43-37509 thru 43-39508
	39-1 thru 39-10	B-17G-DL	42-3483 thru 42-3563
B-17C	40-2042 thru 40-2079		42-37714 thru 42-38213
B-17D	40-3059 thru 40-3100		42-106984 thru 42-107233
B-17E	41-2393 thru 41-2669		44-6001 thru 44-7000
	41-9011 thru 41-9245		44-83236 thru 44-83885
B-17F-BO	41-24340 thru 41-24639	B-17G-VE	42-39758 thru 42-40057
	42-5050 thru 42-5484		42-97436 thru 42-98035
	42-29467 thru 42-31031		44-8001 thru 44-9000

	44-85492 thru 44-85841
XB-40	41-24341
YB-40	42-5732 thru 42-5744
	42-5871
	42-5920 and 42-5921
	42-5923 thru 42-5925
	42-5927
TB-40	42-5833 and 42-5834
	42-5872
	42-5926

World War II B-17 Combat Units

Pacific

Group	Squadrons	Period
19	14, 28, 30, 92, 435	Dec. 1941 to late 1942
7	9, 11, 22, 436	Dec. 1941 to late 1942
11	26, 42, 98, 431	Dec. 1941 to late 1942
43	63, 64, 65, 403	Feb. 1942 to Sep. 1943
5	23, 31, 72, 394	Dec. 1941 to late 1942

Eighth, Twelfth and Fifteenth Air Forces

Group	Squadrons	Period
97	340, 341, 342, 414	Aug. 1942 to May 1945
301	32, 352, 353, 419	Sep. 1942 to May 1945

Twelfth and Fifteenth Air Forces

Group	Squadrons	Period
2	11, 49, 91, 429	Apr. 1943 to May 1945
99	346, 347, 348, 416	Mar. 1943 to May 1945

Fifteenth Air Force

Group	Squadrons	Period
463	772, 773, 774, 775	Mar. 1944 to May 1945
483	815, 816, 817, 840	Apr. 1994 to May 1945

Eighth Air Force

Group	Squadrons	Period
91	322, 323, 324, 401	Nov. 1942 to May 1945
92	325, 326, 327, 407	Sep. 1942 to May 1945
94	331, 332, 333, 410	May 1943 to May 1945
95	334, 335, 336, 412	May 1943 to May 1945
96	337, 338, 339, 413	May 1943 to May 1945
100	349, 350, 351, 418	Jun. 1943 to May 1945
303	358, 359, 360, 427	Nov. 1942 to May 1945
305	364, 365, 366, 422	Nov. 1942 to May 1945
306	367, 368, 369, 423	Oct. 1942 to May 1945
351	408, 409, 410, 411	May 1943 to May 1945
379	524, 525, 526, 527	May 1943 to May 1945
381	532, 533, 534, 535	Jun. 1943 to May 1945
384	544, 545, 546, 547	Jun. 1943 to May 1945
385	548, 549, 550, 551	Jul. 1943 to May 1945
388	560, 561, 562, 563	Jul. 1943 to May 1945
390	568, 569, 570, 571	Aug. 1943 to May 1945
398	600, 601, 602, 603	May 1944 to May 1945
401	612, 613, 614, 615	Nov. 1943 to May 1945
447	708, 709, 710, 711	Dec. 1943 to May 1945
452	728, 729, 730, 731	Feb. 1944 to May 1945
457	748, 749, 750, 751	Feb. 1944 to May 1945
34*	4, 7, 18, 391	Sep. 1994 to May 1945
486*	832, 833, 834, 835	Aug. 1944 to May 1945
487*	836, 837, 838, 839	Aug. 1944 to May 1945
490*	848, 849, 850, 851	Aug. 1944 to May 1945
493*	860, 861, 862, 863	Sep. 1944 to May 1945

* These units entered combat as B-24 groups. Converted to B-17s in months shown.

Other Eighth Air Force B-17 Units

36th Bomb Squadron (radio countermeasures squadron), 1944-1945

5th Air Sea Rescue Squadron, 1944-1945

3rd Air Division Headquarters Flight, 1944-1945

1st Air Division Headquarters Flight, 1944- 1945

Appendix IV

Notable B-17 Survivors

Notable B-17 Survivors

Model	Serial	Location
B-17F	41-24485	Mud Island Museum, Memphis, Tennessee. Memphis Belle static display.
B-17F	42-29782	Museum of Flight, Boeing Field, Seattle, Washington. Static display.
B-17G	42-32076	USAF Museum, Wright-Patterson AFB, Ohio. Shoo Shoo Baby static display.
B-17G	44-83575	Bob Collings/Collings Foundation, Stowe, Massachusetts. Flies as 231909, Nine-O-Nine.
B-17G	43-38635	USAF Museum, Castle AFB, California. Displayed as 38635, Virgin's Delight.
B-17G	44-6393	USAF Museum, March AFB, California. Displayed as 230092, Second Patches.
B-17G	44-8543	Dr. William D. Hospers/B. C. Vintage Flying Machines, Ft. Worth Texas. Flies as 48543 Chuckie.
B-17G	44-83512	USAF Museum, Lackland AFB, Texas. Displayed as 483512 Heavens Above.
B-17G	44-83514	Confederate Air Force, Mesa, Arizona. Flies as 483514, Sentimental Journey.
B-17G	44-83546	Military Aircraft Restoration Corporation, Chino, California. Loaned to March AFB Museum, California.
B-17G	44-83684	Planes of Fame, Chino, California. Displayed as 483684, Picadilly Lily.
B-17G	44-83785	Evergreen Equity, McMinnville, Oregon. Flies as 483785.
B-17G	44-83872	Confederate Air Force, Midland, Texas. Flies as 483872, Texas Raider.
B-17G	55-83884	Eighth Air Force Museum, Barksdale, AFB, Louisiana. Displayed as 38289, Yankee Doodle II.
B-17G	44-85599	Dynes AFB Museum, Abilene, Texas. Displayed as 48559.
B-17G	44-85718	Lone Star Flight Museum, Galveston, Texas. Flies as 238050, Thunderbird.
B-17G	44-85740	EAA Aviation Foundation, Oshkosh, Wisconsin. Flies as 85740, Aluminum Overcast.
B-17G	44-85778	Warbirds of Great Britain, Bournemouth, England. To fly as Sally A.
B-17G	44-85784	B-17 Preservation Trust, Duxford, England. Flies as 24485, Sally B.
B-17G	44-83559	UAAF Museum, Offutt AFB, Nebraska. Displayed as 23474, King Bee.
B-17G	44-83563	National Warplane Museum, Genesco, New York. Flies as 297400, Fuddy Duddy.
B-17G	44-85228	USAF Museum, Pima County Air Museum, Tucson, Arizona. Displayed as 231892, I'll Be Around.
B-17G	44-85829	Yankee Air Force, Willow Run, Michigan. To fly as 485829, Yankee Lady.

Index